FIREPLACE DESIGNS

DUE DATE			

Also by Gerald L. Weaver:
Structural Detailing for Technicians

FIREPLACE DESIGNS

GERALD L. WEAVER

BETTERWAY BOOKS
CINCINNATI, OHIO

Cover photograph by Pam Monfort
Typography by Park Lane Associates

97 96 95 94 93   5 4 3 2 1

Library of Congress Cataloging-in-Publication Data

Weaver, Gerald L.
    Fireplace designs : great fireplaces of yesterday, today, and tomorrow / Gerald L. Weaver. -- 1st ed.
      p. cm.
    Includes index.
    ISBN 1-55870-281-4 : $14.95
    1. Fireplaces. I. Title.
TH7425.W32 1993
697'.1--dc20
                                                         92-38666
                                                         CIP

This book is dedicated to my wife, Joan (who typed the manuscript), and to my two stepsons, Chris and Ty, all of whom share my enjoyment of our own fireplaces. It is also dedicated to my parents, the late Gerald N. Weaver and Vina V. Weaver, who have always provided me with encouragement for the many projects I have undertaken.

Acknowledgments

The author gratefully acknowledges the valuable assistance provided by the following companies that furnished current fireplace and fireplace product information:

Heatilator, Inc.
Division of Hon Industries
1915 W. Saunders Street
Mt. Pleasant, IA 52641

Majestic Division
Equus Building Products, L.P.
1000 E. Market Street
Huntington, IN 46750

Marco Mfg., Inc.
2520 Industry Way
Lynwood, CA 90262

Preface

*I*n reading this book, and thereby expressing an interest in fireplaces, I believe that you have become a kindred spirit. I am not alone in being drawn to the fireplace, as a moth is drawn to a flame. A cheery fire must satisfy some deeply ingrained primal need, while imparting a feeling of security and well-being. After all, what else can relax, entertain, mesmerize, and yes, occasionally put us in a semi-comatose state, any better than a brisk fire and welcoming hearth?

At fireside can come, almost unbidden, the most creative of thoughts, the most colorful memories of good times and good friends, the most enlightening and enjoyable of conversations, and the most intimate moments of sharing and expressing love. Indeed, the fireplace can evoke in each of us the desire and the ability to think lofty thoughts, awaken the muse of poetry, and entice us to wax philosophical.

There are few developments of our early forebears that have endured, updated but virtually unchanged, for so very, very many years. The fireplace seems still to retain its appeal to a wide variety of people. As you read this, it is not hard to imagine that a cowboy somewhere is crouched in front of a fireplace in some drafty line shack or high country cabin. I can picture a couple in evening dress, back from the opera, seated in authentic period furniture, warming themselves in front of a formal marble-fronted fireplace; or a younger couple in designer clothes, enjoying their designer fireplace while sitting on their designer couch; and most certainly, the worker in coveralls enjoying his brick or stone fireplace from the comfort of his recliner.

You may elect to view the fireplace only as a heating device, a back-up or emergency heater, a place to hang Christmas stockings, or as the focal point and *piéce de résistance* of your home. I certainly respect your right to those opinions. I, however, will continue to revere and pay homage to this enduring and faithful friend of man.

It is my hope that the information and designs that follow will be of inspiration and use to you as you set about creating your own fireplace. You will excuse me, I'm sure, if I return now to my own insistently beckoning hearth.

Contents

Chapter 1

Evolution of the Fireplace

Prehistoric man utilized fire for cooking and warmth in the simplest possible way, first as an open fire (sometimes contained within a circle of loose stones), and eventually as an open fire adjacent to the rock wall of his cave dwelling. Thousands of years later, crude, simple huts were developed, and the open fire was moved to a central location inside the hut. Living in an enclosed space offered numerous advantages, but the smoke from the fire presented problems for the inhabitants. Their solution was a simple one. They had observed that smoke rises, so they created a hole in the roof to permit the rising smoke to exit.

Various types of construction were used for early huts, and most incorporated materials that were either flammable or easily damaged by fire. One type used in many parts of the world is referred to as "wattle" construction. It relied on a lightweight structure of limbs and tree branches, interlocked much like a beaver lodge, with grass and mud applied to both interior and exterior surfaces. These structures were primarily dome-shaped, and the hole for smoke exit was at the top and in the center of the dome. Examples of this style are still present in Australia, Africa, and on some American Indian reservations.

The Plains Indians, often nomadic in nature, used straight tree branches or saplings, laced together with rawhide at the top (forming a pyramidal or conical frame) and covered with animal skins. The skin covering was lapped near the top with a flap that could be pulled aside to form the "smoke hole." The "tepee," or "tipi," thus constructed permitted the owner to take it down, transport it to a new location, and reassemble it. The fire in the tepee was placed, as in the case of the hut, in the center of the enclosed space.

CENTRAL HEARTHS

The placement of the fire in a central location continued to be common practice until the sixteenth century. Contrary to what might naturally be assumed, the *raised hearth* is not a development of recent years. The early central hearths were frequently raised above floor level, making fire-tending easier, facilitating cooking without so much bending over, and providing built-in seating for the inhabitants. During the later years of extensive use of the central hearth, the smoke hole in the roof was fitted with a device to assist with controlling the effects of wind and to provide protection of the building's interior from rain. These assemblies, called *smoke louvers*, were hollow, ventilated devices, resembling the cupola for attic ventilation used today. (See Figure 1.)

The years of the central-hearth fireplace brought the development of the first *andirons*. Primarily viewed as decorative or ornamental items now, andirons were created to assist with cooking and fire building. Metal andirons in their functional form consisted of two vertical bars on flat or arched leg bases, with an elevated horizontal cross-brace to space them apart and keep them upright. The cross-brace served as a log brace, with firewood leaned against it from both sides. The upper part of the vertical members featured extended prongs or notches. This gave the support for a horizontal rod, or *spit*, for cooking meat, and it provided a means of hanging cooking pots directly over the fire. (See Figure 2.)

WALL FIREPLACES

Improved types of construction using stone or adobe materials permitted placing fireplaces against a wall. Also, the first successful attempts to construct buildings of two or more stories precluded the hole in the roof, which was so necessary for the central hearth. The first *wall fireplaces* were constructed without chimneys. They used an extended masonry or metal hood over the fire. Smoke exited through a simple hole through the wall, inside and near the top of the hood. Early fireplaces of this type had no sides or other devices to form a *firebox*. The open fire was simply built against the wall below the hood. (See Figure 3.)

The use of wall fireplaces did not dictate which wall they needed to occupy, so both side wall and end wall locations were used. Many fireplaces of the "wall" type were located in a corner of a room. This practice was common in parts of Europe and particularly popular in Germany and the Scandinavian countries. (See Figure 4.)

CHIMNEYS AND FLUES

The first crude efforts were eventually adapted to create *chimneys* or *flues* to channel the unwanted smoke more efficiently from the fireplace directly to the outdoors. The easiest location for constructing the flue was against a wall or in a corner, and occupants were already building their wall fireplaces in those locations. The emerging wall fireplace, with its flue and chimney structure, offered several new advantages. The masonry surface behind the fire aided the process of radiating heat, and the heavy mass of masonry in the wall and the chimney stored heat from the fire, thus increasing its efficiency.

Early fireplaces had inherent disadvantages, such as being prone to downdrafts and the actual leakage of smoke through cracks and open joints in flue materials. As construction expertise increased and the problems were more clearly studied, the concepts of *smoke shelves* (to temper effects of downdrafts) and *dampers* emerged. The damper was made possible through development of successful methods of fabricating cast iron and steel. Since cast iron relied on bolted joints, smoke still leaked through. Steel and the welding process provided much better fireplace components. (See Figure 5.)

Bricks made their way to America in the later years of the eighteenth century and became available in a variety of sizes and shapes. Brick permitted much more control in fireplace construction and allowed building with much more precise dimensions. Early experiments in making brick led to a method to create *firebrick* for use in the actual firebox. Firebrick was durable, whereas simple clay brick had a tendency to crack and deteriorate from the intense heat. Flues were made more durable and more tight with the emergence of fired-clay pipe or *flue liners*. (See Figure 6.)

EARLY FIREPLACE DESIGNERS

Many different people in various parts of the world contributed to the development, refinement, and changing design of the fire place. Certainly among those contributing most were Dutch scientist and engineer Jan Ingenhousz and America's Benjamin Franklin. Experiments by, and the design work of, Massachusetts-born Benjamin Thompson led to the type of fireplace closest to the present day configuration. Thompson left his home in Rumford, New Hampshire at an early age, where he served in cabinet positions in Munich, Germany. For all practical purposes, he ruled Bavaria from his cabinet position. He was awarded the title of Count of the Holy Roman Empire, and he chose to be called Count Rumford, after his home town of Rumford, New Hampshire.

After ten years in Munich, Thompson moved to London and devoted himself to improving fireplace design. He based his designs on brick and made fireplaces smaller and more shallow, utilizing fireboxes with narrow backs and wide flaring sides. By sloping the back wall, the narrow opening for smoke escape was placed in a forward position and incorporated a somewhat high smoke shelf. The designs Thompson perfected were known as *Count Rumford Fireplaces*, and the principles they featured are still used, though somewhat modified, in present-day manufactured fireplace units. (See Figure 7.)

FIREPLACES USED FOR COOKING

As mentioned at the beginning of the chapter, through many centuries fire was used as the source for warmth and heat for cooking. Fireplaces were frequently built to provide for both purposes in a single unit. This, of course, meant fireplaces with large face openings, large hearths, and large flues. Ovens were frequently incorporated on one side, and arms, or *cranes*, of metal, pivoted to positions directly over the fire to support the bail, or handle, of kettles and other cooking utensils. (See Figure 8.)

Colonial fireplaces were often of large proportions, with face openings of six- to eight-foot widths. It is erroneous to assume that fires were built to fill these huge fireplaces. Rather, a moderate-sized fire was built in the center, with the sides used for the oven and access to cooking utensils. Because of the generous dimensions of the fireplaces, large hand-hewn log beams could be used for the *lintel* over the opening, which supported the brick or stone above without danger of igniting from the heat of the fire. It should be remembered that these early fireplaces were constructed prior to the availability of steel angle iron or "I" beams.

Many homeowners abandoned the fireplace as a means of cooking with the emergence in the eighteenth century of manufactured stoves. Led by the development of Benjamin Franklin's namesake, the *Franklin Stove*, other types of cast iron stoves became available, including the *potbelly* stove and the massive *kitchen range*. The advantages offered by the stoves included increased radiation from the heated cast iron surfaces, better draft for more efficient burning, and successful operable dampers to regulate the fire. (See Figure 9.)

RECENT DEVELOPMENTS

With the elimination of cooking as a function, fireplaces grew smaller and more effective for the purpose of heating. It became apparent that there was an advantageous ratio between the size of the fire and the size of the fireplace. A small fire in a large fireplace was extremely inefficient since it was incapable of warming the adjacent masonry materials to assist in reflecting and radiating heat. Huge fireplaces demand large logs, which are devoured voraciously. Dwellings were becoming tighter due to better materials and construction techniques, and smaller fireplaces became more appropriate to satisfy the heating needs of the occupants. (See Figure 10.)

Our present century has seen the development, manufacture, and widespread use of the double-walled steel *heat-circulating* fireplace unit. These units supplement the heat radiated directly from the fire by drawing air into the space between the two walls where it is heated and circulated back into the room. Typically, the air is drawn in through grilles at, or near, floor level, and the heated air (which rises) is discharged into the room through grilles (or registers) near ceiling height. The circulation of air through the unit and into the room can be enhanced with the addition of low velocity electric fans, which are an option available from the manufacturer. (See Figure 11.)

The basic heat-circulating fireplace units do require masonry materials surrounding the unit along with a firebrick hearth since the unit has no bottom, and temperatures of the unit are high when it is being used. Typically, the temperature of the outer steel walls will exceed 450 degrees for the portion housing the fire, and 320 degrees for the section containing the damper and the flue transition. It is easy to understand how these units are capable of heating large volumes of air when the surface area of steel plates directly surrounding the fire varies from 2,600 square inches upward, depending on the size of the fireplace unit's face opening. (See Figure 12.)

The desire for safe, efficient fireplace units led designers and engineers to the development of the factory-built, so-called *zero clearance* fireplace unit. These units eliminate the need for masonry materials and the massive foundations and footings necessary for their support. Both fireplace and flues are multiple-walled steel assemblies, which circulate air through some spaces to cool the outer surfaces. In addition, the units are insulated to prevent heat loss to their exterior. Pre-built units are available in both "radiant only" and "heat circulating" configurations. Most such units have thin, high-temperature refractory material (molded with a brick pattern) on the visible side, back, and bottom surfaces of the fire chamber. (See Figure 13.)

Fireplaces have indeed come a long way from their crude "open fire" origins to the safe, efficient units of today. The heavy masonry materials used previously are no longer necessary. The amount of space required has been dramatically reduced, and the amount of labor for construction or installation has been significantly reduced as well. Problems of downdrafts and "smoking" are curtailed when today's units are properly installed. The units lend themselves easily to both new construction and remodeling projects. Current fireplaces provide the inherent "charm" always associated with a fireplace, while serving as an efficient and usable source of heat.

Figure 1. Early smoke louvers.

Figure 2. Early andirons.

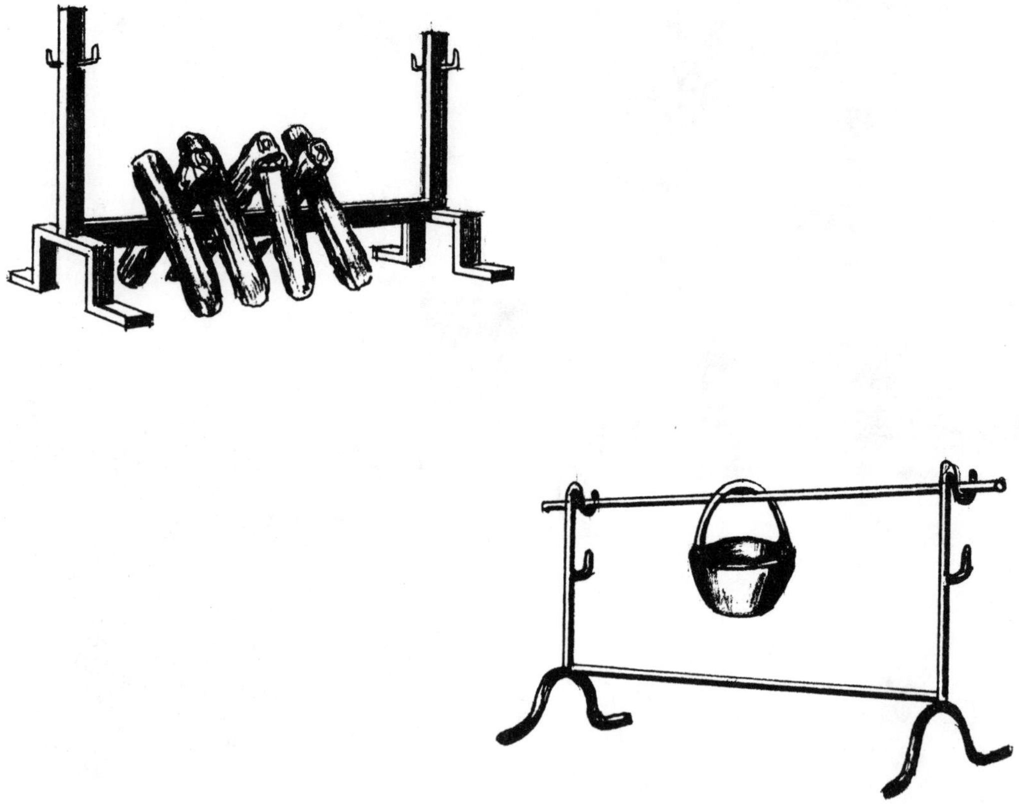

Figure 3. Early hood with slanted smoke hole.

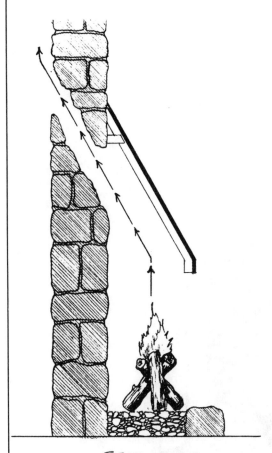

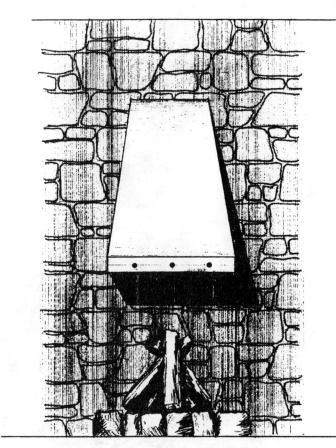

SECTION

FRONT VIEW

Figure 4. Early European corner fireplace.

Figure 5. Smoke shelf and damper.

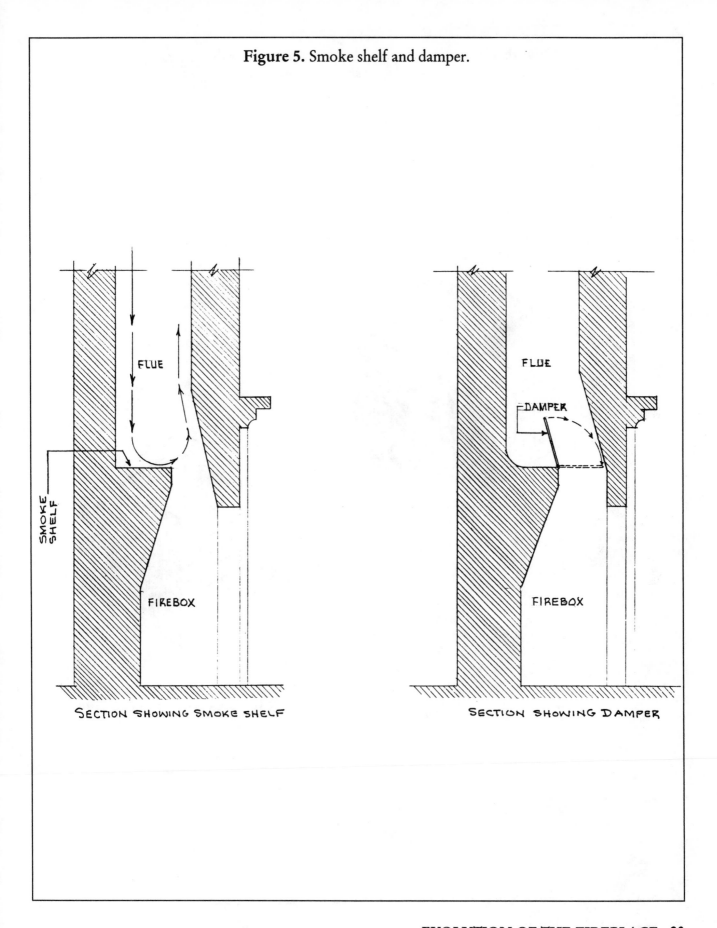

FLUE

SMOKE SHELF

FIREBOX

SECTION SHOWING SMOKE SHELF

FLUE

DAMPER

FIREBOX

SECTION SHOWING DAMPER

Figure 6. Brick chimney and brick chimney with flue liner.

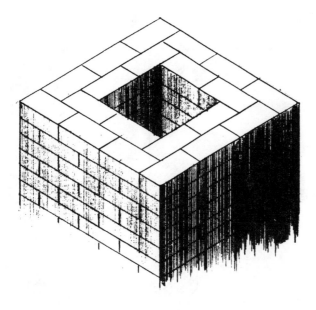

BRICK CHIMNEY

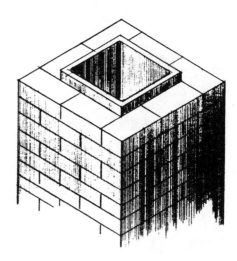

CHIMNEY WITH FLUE LINER

Figure 7. Rumford-type fireplace.

Figure 8. Early fireplace with cooking crane and oven.

Figure 9. Franklin stove and wood-burning range.

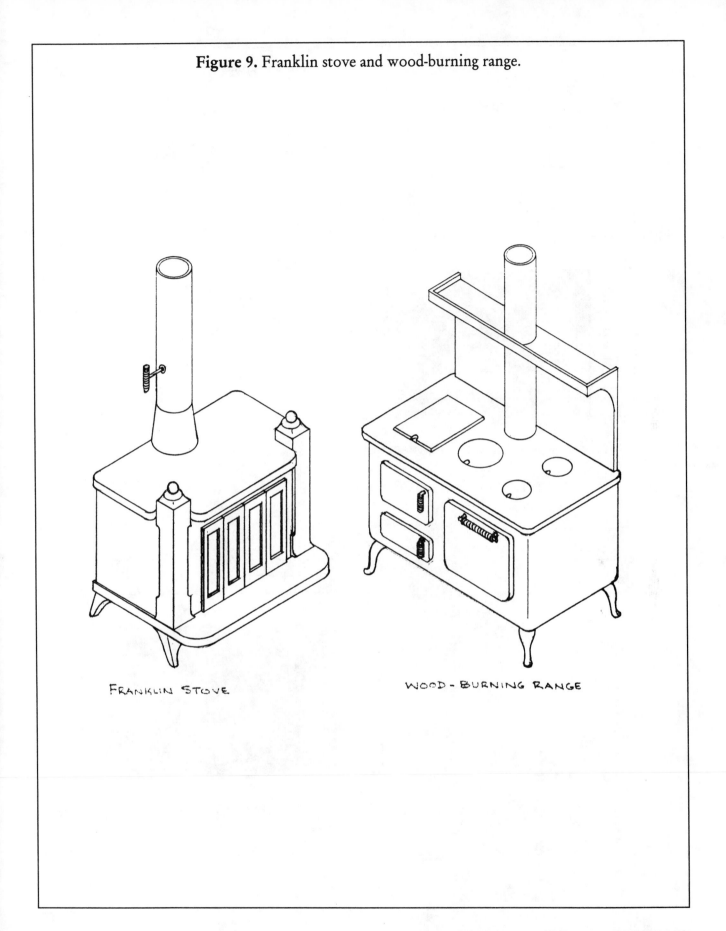

FRANKLIN STOVE

WOOD-BURNING RANGE

Figure 10. Small and large fires in a fireplace.

FIRE TOO SMALL FOR THE FIREPLACE

FIRE LARGE ENOUGH TO CONTRIBUTE HEAT

Figure 11. Heat-circulating fireplace unit.

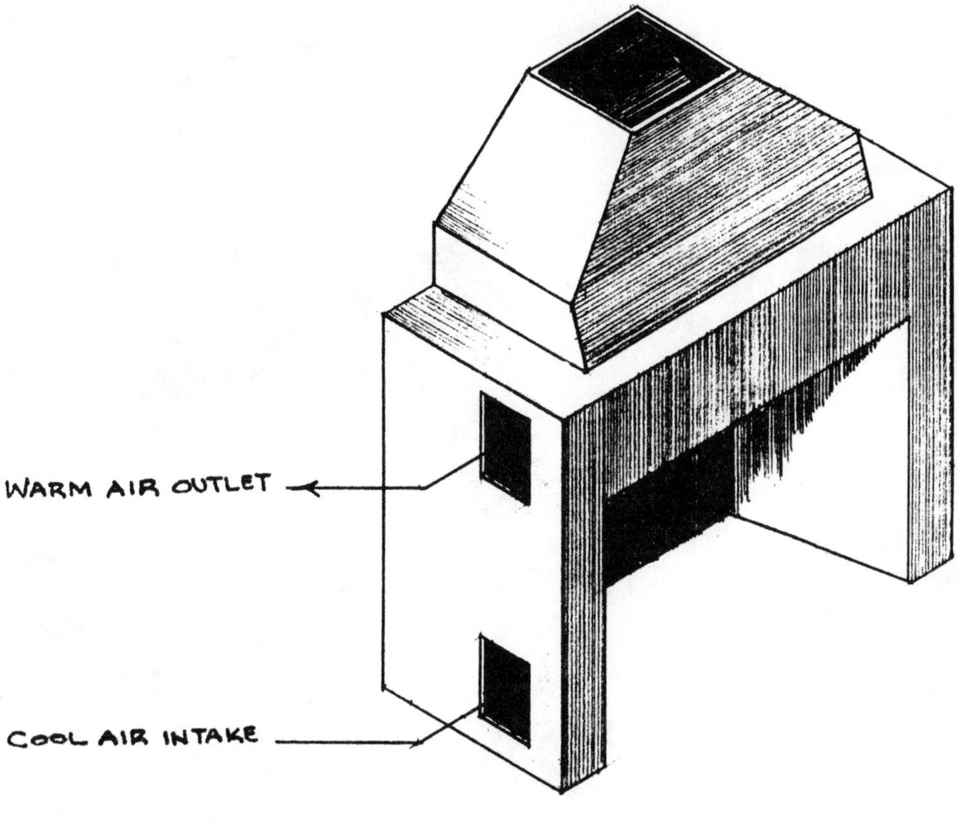

WARM AIR OUTLET

COOL AIR INTAKE

Figure 12. Outside surface temperatures on heat-circulating unit.

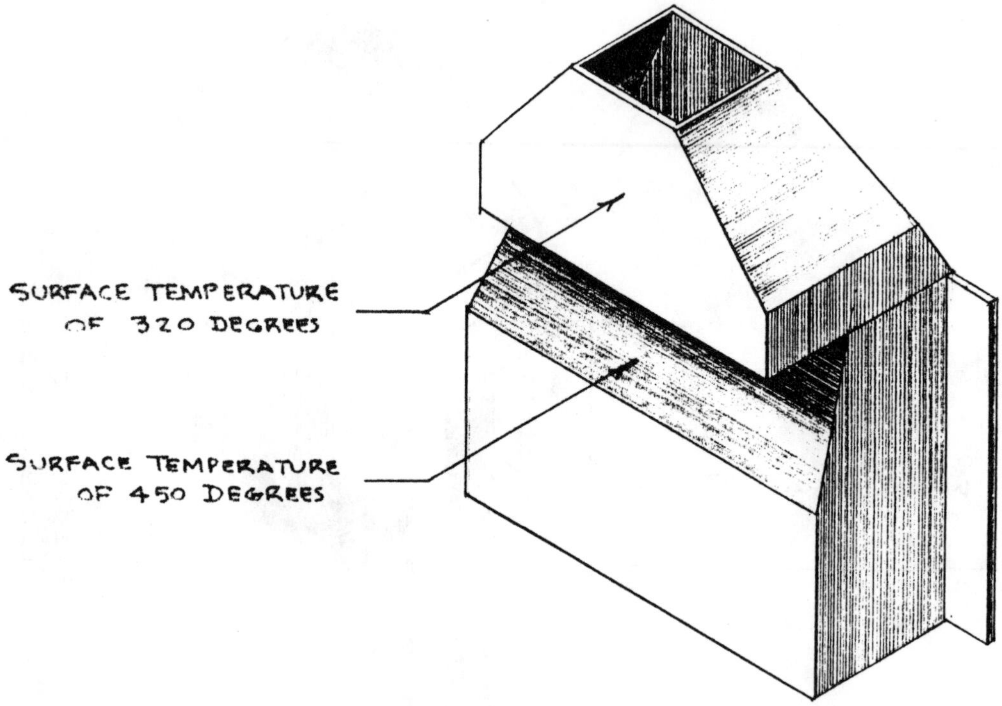

SURFACE TEMPERATURE
OF 320 DEGREES

SURFACE TEMPERATURE
OF 450 DEGREES

Figure 13. Radiant pre-built unit and heat-circulating unit with flue section.

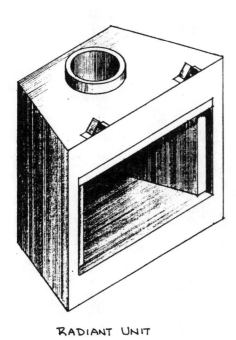

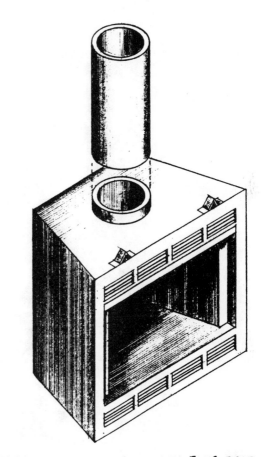

RADIANT UNIT

HEAT - CIRCULATING UNIT WITH FLUE SECTION

Chapter 2

How Fireplaces Work

No difference exists in the way the open fires of our primitive ancestors burned and the way fires in present-day fireplaces burn. A fire must draw oxygen from the air in order to support combustion. As soon as the first-lit flames start to flicker, the air above them is warmed, and since warm air rises, an upward-moving current of air is created. The upward travel of the warm air, along with the consumption of the wood fuel, creates a pull of new air into the fire, thus establishing an ongoing cycle. In a fireplace, once the fire has had time to heat the smoke chamber and flue, the smoke chamber and flue help to increase the upward pull of warm air and smoke. (See Figure 14.)

Before the fire is burning well, the first smoke drawn into the smoke chamber tends to linger there. The flue, because it is not sufficiently warm, tends to create a downdraft, rather than drawing the air and smoke upward. The downdraft shelf in today's fireplace prevents the smoke from being blown back into the firebox. It is instead induced to swirl into the upward-moving warm air current being created by the fire. Once the fire is burning well, the natural draft takes care of the problem.

Once a good fire is underway, the heated firebox, smoke chamber, and flue work together to sustain an updraft which works for, rather than against, the fire's function. The fire gives off heat in three different ways. Some of the heat goes up the flue with the smoke. A large amount of the heat is given off to the room by *convection* since air currents close to the firebox circulate along with room air. The largest contribution of the fireplace's heat occurs as *radiation*. In other words, heat rays from the glowing embers and flames are reflected (or bounced) off the sides and back of the firebox and into the room. (See Figure 15).

Early homes had cracks and joints that permitted cold outside air to enter the house. This, of course, meant uncomfortable drafts. The early inhabitants understood very clearly that sitting in front of the fireplace (where the radiated heat could reach them) was the best way to get warm. Their desire to escape the cool drafts in the room even lead to the development of the "winged" chair, which protected them from drafts from behind as well as from both sides. (See Figure 16.)

Air, as mentioned earlier, is necessary if the fire is to burn and the fireplace is to function. Early construction leaked enough air naturally to fulfill that purpose. The constant quest for tighter, more energy-efficient buildings eventually resulted in houses so tight that fireplaces could not operate properly, and heating and water heating equipment were affected as well. A health hazard was posed by the over-consumption of the limited oxygen in the house, and the presence of flue gases from equipment that could not burn with a clean flame. Occupants were forced to leave windows ajar or to install adjustable louvers through walls in order to draw in adequate quantities of new, oxygen-rich air. (See Figure 17.)

Residences are currently tight and energy efficient and employ better methods to provide fresh air intake. Building codes now frequently require that measures be provided for just that purpose. Furnace rooms are generally either equipped with ducts to bring outside air into the room or equipped with flues that feature multiple walls, allowing one of the spaces to bring outside air into the room from above the roof line. Many heating systems have fresh air intake ducts with operable dampers, which can be set to introduce measured amounts of fresh air. Fireplace unit manufacturers have addressed the fresh air intake problem with units that include ducts to provide outside air directly into the firebox or multiple wall flues that pull fresh air in from roof level. (See Figure 18.)

Fireplaces consist of several basic components, whether they are job-built (conventional) or the more recent factory-built units. Although many of these components have been mentioned earlier, it may be helpful to list each, with a brief description, and the accompanying illustration.

FIREPLACE COMPONENTS

The Firebox

The chamber that actually contains the fire is referred to as the firebox. In a conventional masonry fireplace, it is constructed with firebrick, while manufactured units use heavy steel. The sides slant outward, and the upper portion of the back slopes upward and forward. This configuration is intended to reflect the greatest possible amount of heat into the room.

The Hearth

The bottom of the firebox is the hearth. Since it is the area on which the fire is built, it is again built with firebrick in the conventional fireplace. Pre-built units use heavy steel for this surface, often covered with a layer of refractory material. Frequently, the entire fireproof surface, both inside the firebox and extending into the room, is referred to as the hearth. To be technically correct, the portion extending into the room should be called the *extended hearth*. It provides protection from sparks and embers escaping from the firebox. Some sources use the terms *back hearth* and *front hearth* for these surfaces. (See Figure 19.)

The Throat

Smoke must have a path to make its exit from the firebox. The opening, or passage, from the firebox to the smoke chamber is called the throat. By slanting the upper portion of the rear firebox wall forward, the throat is positioned in front of the center of the firebox. The opening for the throat is created in the brickwork of the conventional fireplace and is formed with steel plates in pre-built fireplace units.

The Damper

It is advantageous to be able to vary the size of the throat opening for different conditions and to be able to close it completely when the fireplace is not in use. This prevents warm house air from being lost up the flue. The damper is a movable steel flap placed at the fireplace throat. It can be used to control the rate at which the fire is burning by varying the draft up the flue.

The Smoke Chamber

The space from the top of the throat to the bottom of the flue is known as the smoke chamber. It most often has sloping ends, front, and back, which enable it to funnel the smoke from the wider throat into the narrower flue.

The Smoke Shelf

The function of the smoke shelf is twofold. It assists in diverting downdrafts coming down the flue and encourages eddying smoke to be drawn into the air currents rising up the flue. It is, in essence, a horizontal shelf, the same width (side to side) as the throat and extending from the back of the throat to the back of the flue. (See Figure 20.)

The Flue

The hollow tube that permits the smoke to travel from the smoke chamber to the exterior of the home (above the roof line) is called the flue. In conventional fireplace construction, it is often square or rectangular in cross-section, since clay tile flue liners are readily available in those shapes. Most factory-built units require insulated metal flues with circular cross-sections. (See Figure 21.)

The Surround

The area on the front surface of the fireplace, adjacent to the sides and top of the firebox, is frequently called the surround. In building conventional masonry fireplaces, non-combustible materials are required for the surround. Many authorities (building codes, insurance requirements, etc.) have designated that there be a minimum of eight inches of non-combustible materials (tile, brick, etc.) between the firebox and any wood trim. Pre-built zero clearance fireplace units come with their finished metal fronts as part of the unit itself. (See Figures 22 and 23.)

The Chimney

The flue is contained inside of the chimney. The chimney is most often brick or stone in the case of conventional masonry fireplaces. The chimney extends above the roof line and is visible from outside of the house. Many masonry chimneys are made a decorative feature of the house with fancy caps and patterns created in the brickwork. Insulated metal flues of pre-built fireplaces can be enclosed with wood, brick, or many other materials to form the chimney. They are sometimes left exposed since they are weather resistant and smoke- and watertight. (See Figure 24.)

The Mantel

Certainly not a necessary part for the function of the fireplace, the mantel is the horizontal projecting shelf, or ledge, on the front of the finished fireplace above the opening and surround. If it is of wood or other combustible material, the mantel must be placed high enough above the firebox to ensure that it will not catch fire. Codes and fireplace manufacturers' literature strictly designate the minimum safe distances for the specific type of fireplace being constructed or installed. Mantels serve only a decorative purpose; therefore, you will find many styles of fireplace treatments have no mantel at all. (See Figure 25.)

The Flue and Spark Cap

The purpose of a cap, located above the top of the flue, is to assist in preventing downdrafts and to shed rainwater. In addition, many caps include a metal mesh screen designed to prevent potentially dangerous sparks from leaving the flue. Sometimes known as "spark arrestors," these screens are required in some areas, including the state of California. Caps can be constructed on the top of masonry flues and chimneys, and pre-built fireplace units have available a prefabricated metal cap assembly. (See Figure 26.)

The Ash Dump

Many conventional masonry fireplaces have ash dumps, or ash pits, particularly those fireplaces built above a basement or crawlspace. The bottom of the firebox has an opening into a hollow, masonry-enclosed space below. The opening is fitted with a steel lid assembly. Ashes from previous fires can simply be dumped into the lower space to be disposed of later. Access for cleaning out the ash pit is gained through a small steel or cast iron door. If the dwelling has a basement, the clean-out door is located below the fireplace and close to the basement floor. Crawlspace units have the clean-out door on the exterior of the house just above ground level. Due to the danger of introducing live coals and embers into the ash pit, the pit and all of the accompanying accessories need to be of noncombustible materials. (See Figure 27.)

Figure 14. How a fireplace works.

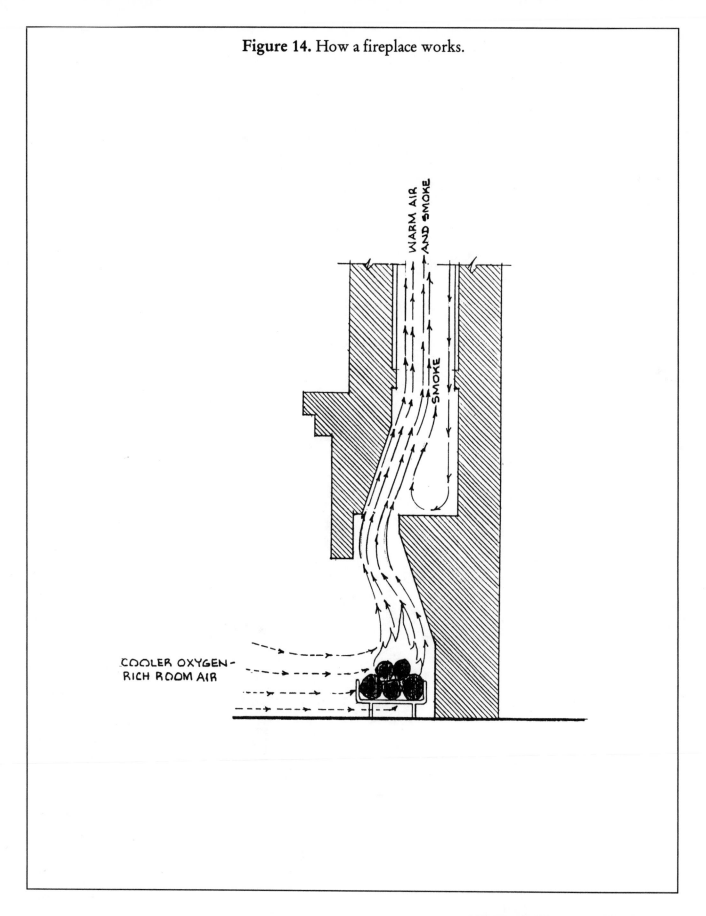

WARM AIR AND SMOKE

SMOKE

COOLER OXYGEN-
RICH ROOM AIR

Figure 15. How a fireplace provides heat.

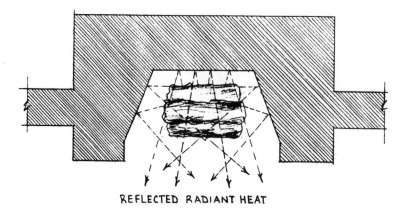

REFLECTED RADIANT HEAT

PLAN VIEW

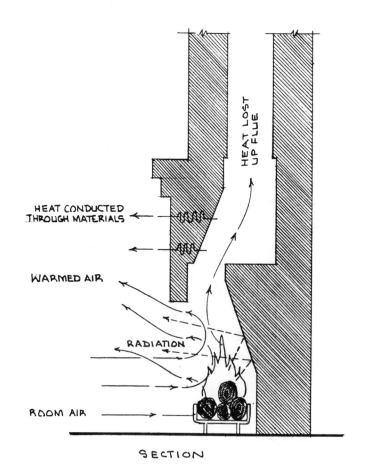

HEAT LOST UP FLUE

HEAT CONDUCTED THROUGH MATERIALS

WARMED AIR

RADIATION

ROOM AIR

SECTION

Figure 16. Winged chair to protect from drafts.

Figure 17. Air drawn to fireplace for combustion.

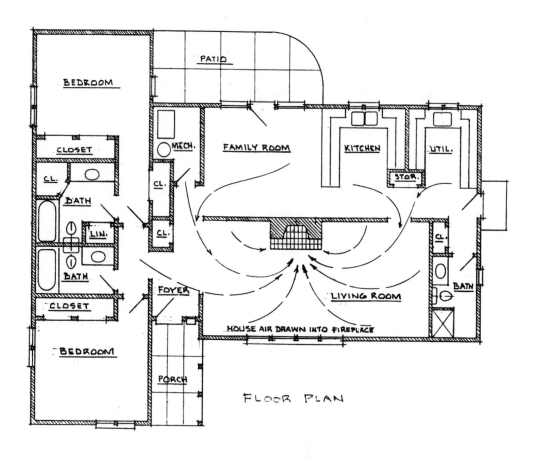

FLOOR PLAN

Figure 18. Fresh air intake methods.

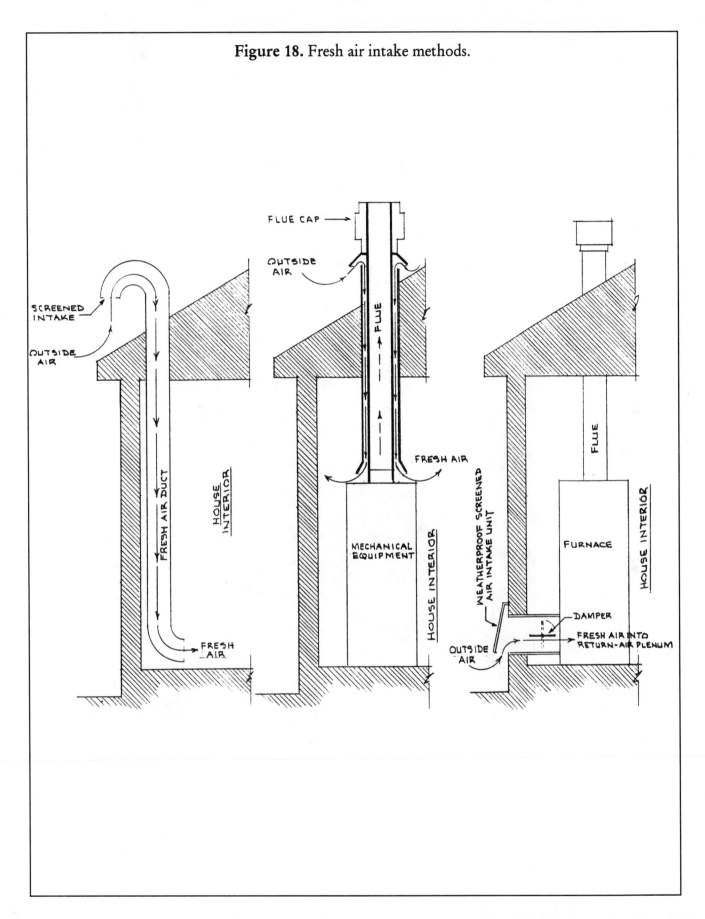

Figure 19. Firebox and hearth.

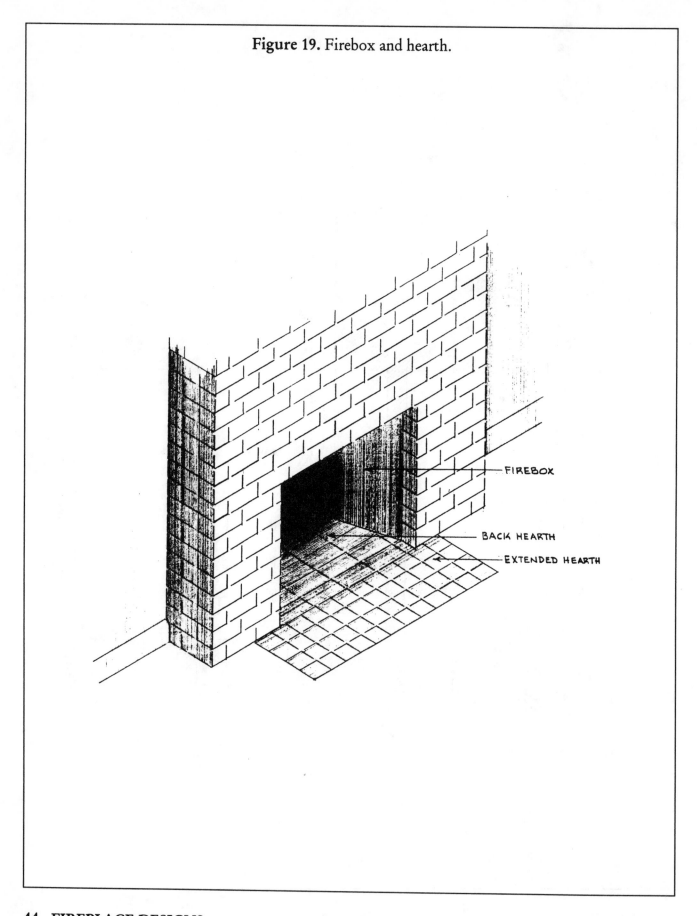

FIREBOX

BACK HEARTH

EXTENDED HEARTH

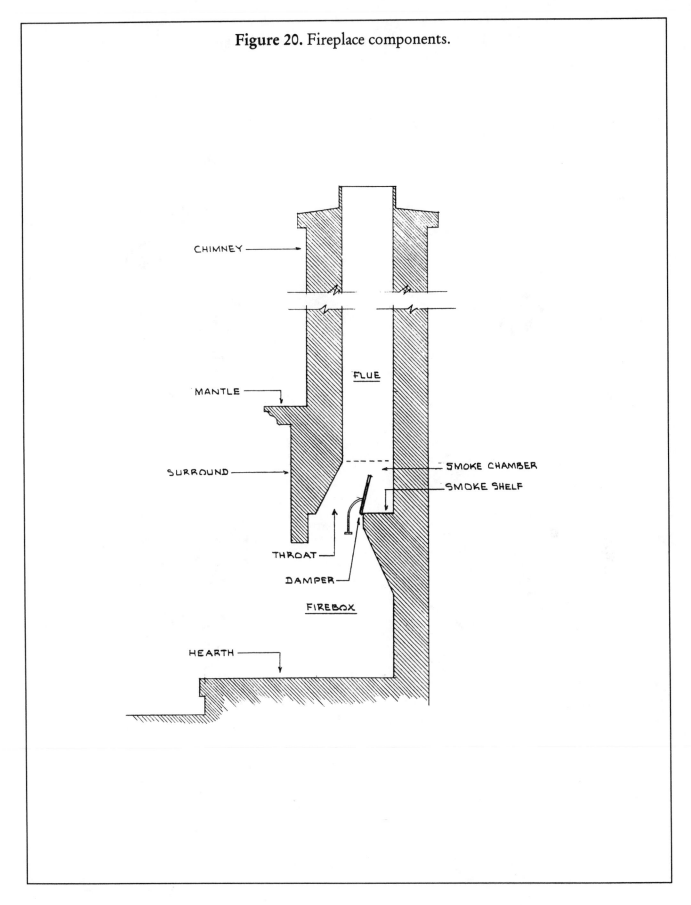

Figure 20. Fireplace components.

Figure 21. Examples of masonry flues and chimneys.

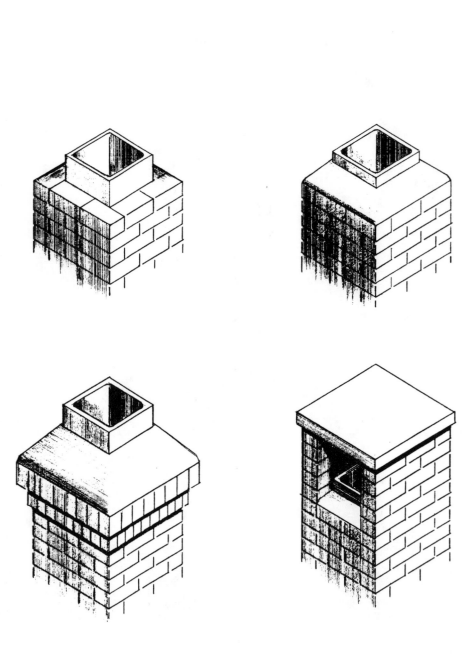

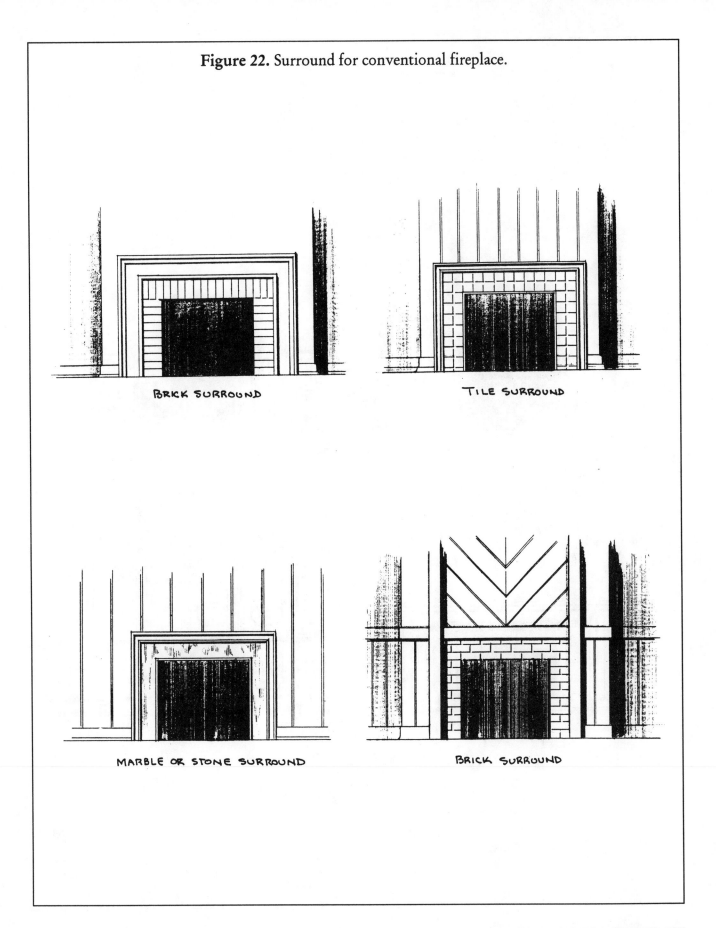

Figure 22. Surround for conventional fireplace.

BRICK SURROUND

TILE SURROUND

MARBLE OR STONE SURROUND

BRICK SURROUND

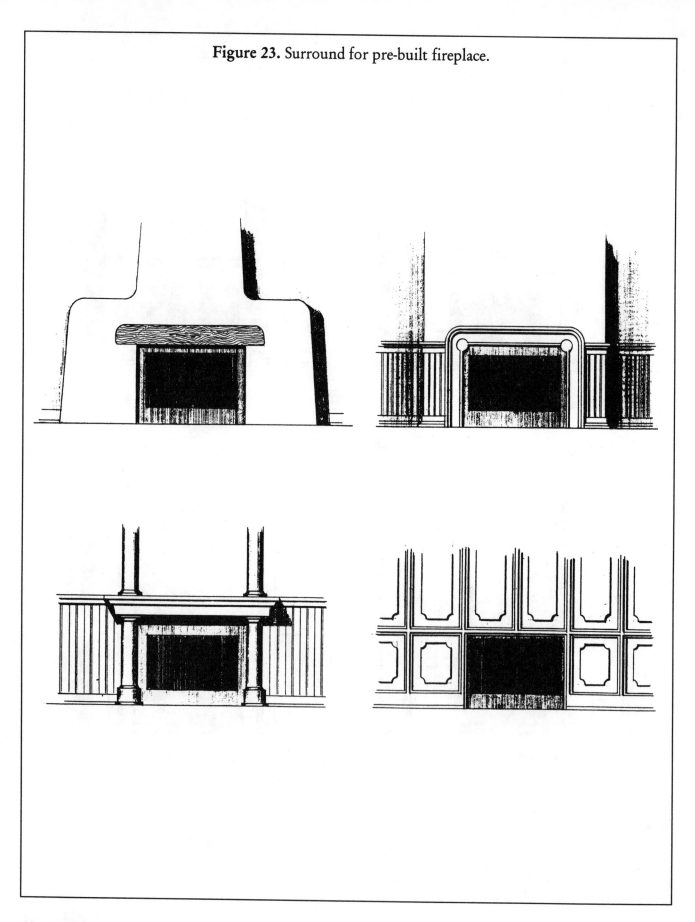

Figure 23. Surround for pre-built fireplace.

Figure 24. Examples of chimney designs.

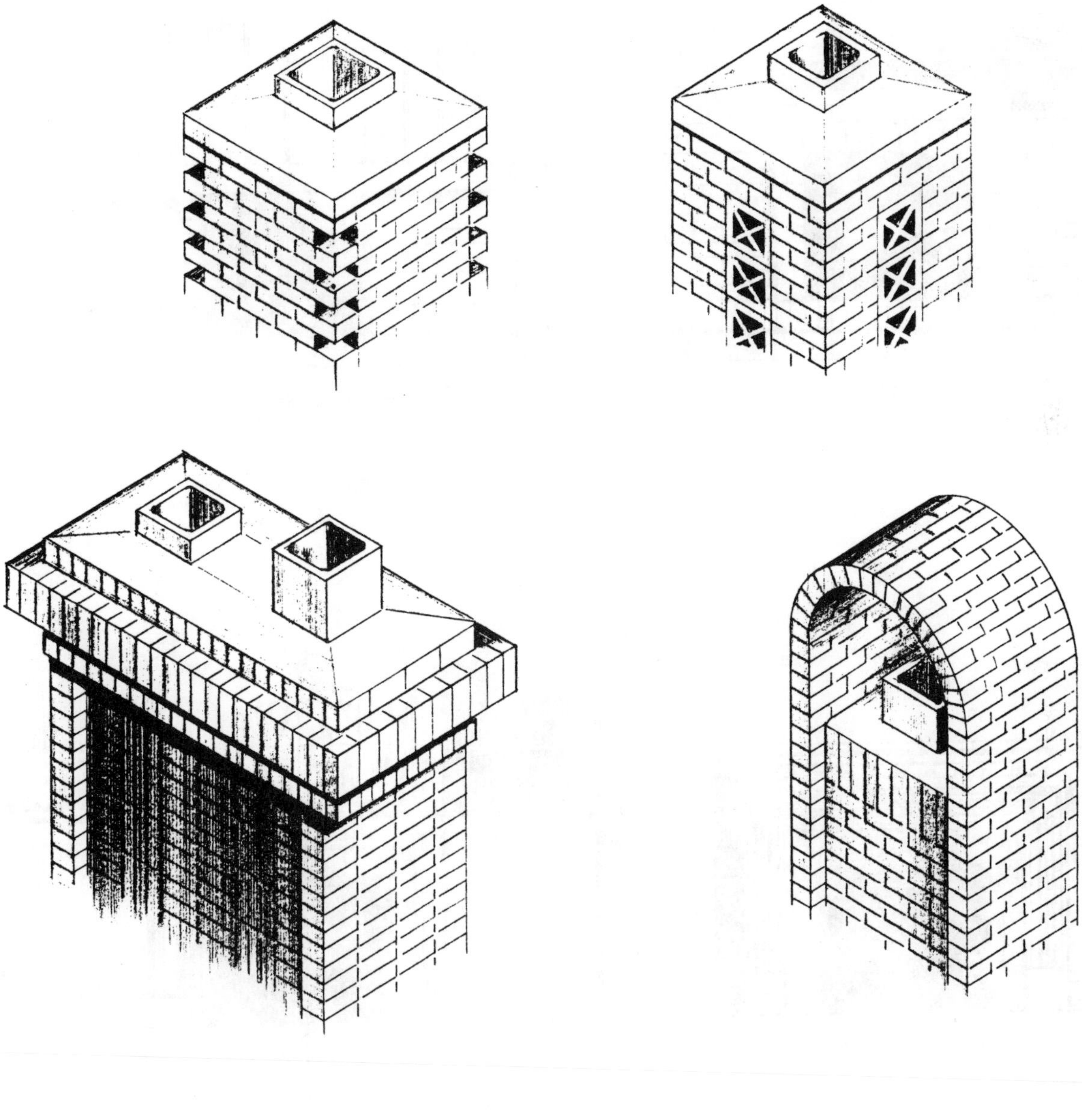

Figure 25. Examples of mantels.

WOOD MANTLE

STONE MANTLE

WOOD MANTLE

WOOD MANTLE AND CABINET TOP

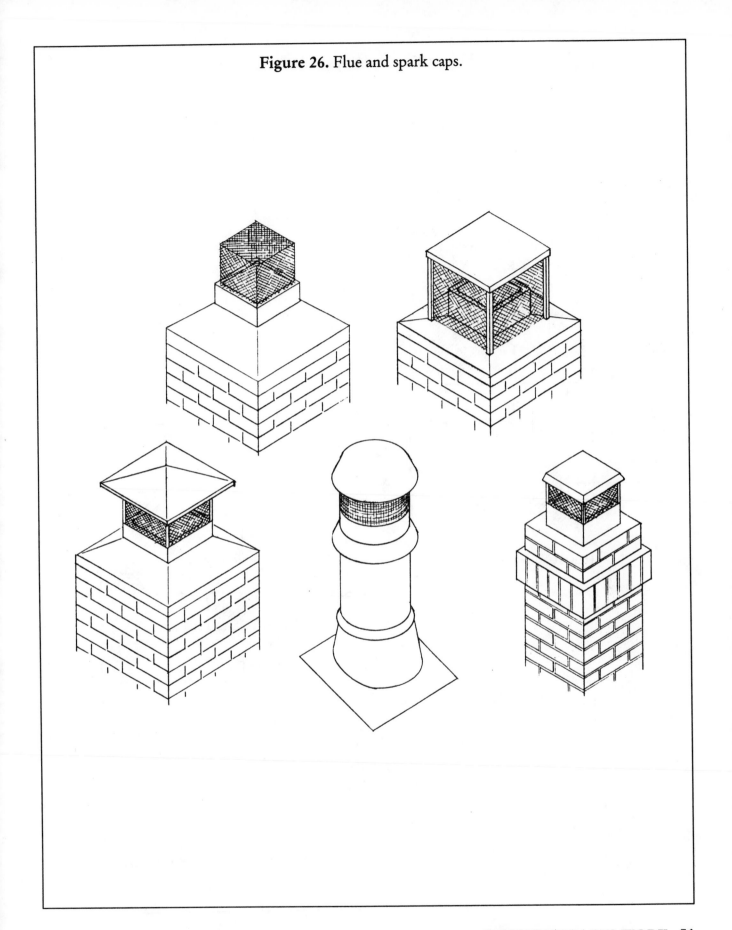

Figure 26. Flue and spark caps.

Figure 27. Ash dumps and ash pits.

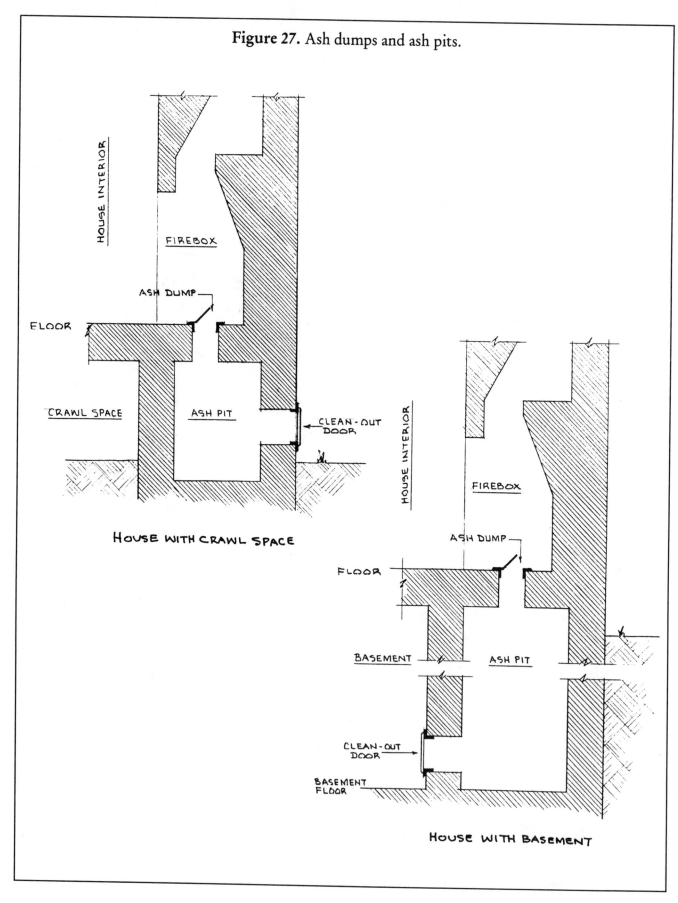

HOUSE INTERIOR

FIREBOX

ASH DUMP

FLOOR

CRAWL SPACE

ASH PIT

CLEAN-OUT DOOR

HOUSE WITH CRAWL SPACE

HOUSE INTERIOR

FIREBOX

ASH DUMP

FLOOR

BASEMENT

ASH PIT

CLEAN-OUT DOOR

BASEMENT FLOOR

HOUSE WITH BASEMENT

Chapter 3

Fireplaces of Today

The fireplaces being constructed today are vastly improved over those built earlier in terms of ease of construction, safety, and operating efficiency. The easy availability of standardized materials and components has been an important contributor to these improvements, and fireplace design criteria provide the guidelines to create truly successful fireplaces. The amount of heat they supply for heating use has increased, while the amount lost has been dramatically reduced. Also, the temperamental smoking fireplace has been practically relegated to the past. Guesswork in fireplace construction has, for the most part, been eliminated.

Today's fireplaces conform basically to two categories. There are still those who prefer a job-built, or built-in-place, fireplace. This type may be one of total masonry construction, with firebrick for the firebox, and utilizing quality steel damper units and accessories. Many job-built fireplaces, featuring heat circulation as well as radiation, use the double-walled manufactured steel fireplace form, which includes damper, throat, downdraft shelf, and smoke dome. The balance of the construction is accomplished with masonry.

Pre-built, or zero clearance, fireplaces provide complete packages, including flues, flashings, caps, etc. With these units, the actual on-site work consists of installation and "cosmetic" treatment of the exposed surfaces surrounding the unit. Some pre-built units require only installation, since they are intended to be free-standing units and have all exterior surfaces already finished.

Pre-built fireplace units have permitted the use of fireplaces in applications where the size and weight of masonry fireplaces previously excluded their use. Fireplaces can now be installed easily in existing homes, in small rooms, and even in modular and mobile homes. There are "packages," or kits, now available specifically for installing pre-built units in mobile homes. Some locations of vacation cabins or summer homes are remote enough that the transportation of heavy masonry materials to the site is difficult and expensive. The pre-built units are ideal for such locations.

Sparsely populated areas often lack the availability of skilled craftsmen and brick masons. Some do-it-yourselfers are skilled enough, or have sufficient courage in lieu of skills, to tackle the task of constructing their own job-built fireplace. Pre-built fireplace units offer the unskilled a simple, well-documented, easy-to-follow installation format, including accompanying step-by-step illustrations, which guide the entire process from start to finish.

This chapter provides more information about both job-built and pre-built units, as well as information about codes and clearances, accessories, and firewood selection.

JOB-BUILT FIREPLACES

Radiant Fireplaces

Earlier chapters discussed job-built masonry fireplaces. Essentially, the firebox and interior hearth are constructed of firebrick to withstand the high heat they encounter. The downdraft or smoke shelf is constructed with common brick, as is the smoke chamber, and common brick surrounds the clay-tile flue liner. The steel damper assembly can be any of several sizes and types. (See Figures 28 and 29.)

Damper units are available in either cast iron or formed steel. They can be purchased with straight ends or sloping ends. The sizes are matched to the finished fireplace width opening desired, and these width openings range generally from twenty-four to sixty inches. A series of dampers is available, called *high-formed dampers*, which also provide the throat and permit a deeper smoke shelf. The method of operation is different for different types of dampers. Dampers are available that have the operating arm, or lever, extended with a circular hole in the end. A fireplace poker is inserted in the hole to close or open the damper by pushing or pulling.

Chain-controlled dampers feature two chains extending below the damper. They are opened by pulling down on one of the chains and closed by pulling down on the other chain. Rotary-controlled dampers are opened or closed by rotating a decorative handle or knob, which projects on the finished face of the fireplace above the firebox opening. Essentially, formed steel damper units are available predominantly with poker-type controls, and a few models with rotary controls. Cast iron damper units are available with chain, rotary, or poker controls.

The brick that forms the firebox of the conventional masonry fireplace must be surrounded with a layer of common brick, thus resulting in a total thickness of eight to nine inches on the sides and back of the firebox. Brick must also be used to surround the clay-tile flue liners. The interior hearth of the firebox is composed of firebrick, most frequently laid "flat" with the largest face exposed. This layer of firebrick must be laid on top of a non-combustible surface and a concrete slab (either poured in place or pre-cast) is used for this purpose.

The decorative appearance of the fireplace is accomplished by surrounding the "functional" fireplace with face brick, stone, drywall, paneling, etc. The mantel, front hearth, and surround finish the installation. As mentioned earlier, code requirements dictate the distance from the fireplace opening to any combustible materials that can be used.

Heat-Circulating Fireplaces

The double-walled heat-circulating fireplace unit is installed on a non-combustible firebrick hearth and is surrounded with two layers of common brick, or one layer of common brick and one layer of face brick. It uses a clay-tile flue liner with brick surrounding the liner. The unit saves considerable construction time, since it incorporates firebox, throat, damper, smoke shelf, and smoke dome in a single pre-built unit. The ductwork for intake and output of air is built into the brickwork, as it is laid around the unit. (See Figures 30 and 31.)

Manufacturers of fireplace components frequently provide charts giving flue sizes and minimum heights of flues for the various sizes of fireplaces. Financing agencies and codes officials also have published criteria. Some much-used rules of thumb indicate that the chimney must extend a minimum of three feet above the high point where the chimney penetrates the roof (for pitched roofs) or four feet above the roof for flat roofs. In addition, the chimney should extend a minimum of two feet above any portion of the building or adjacent structure within ten feet of the chimney location. Codes and recommendations should be referred to prior to any fireplace construction. Current practices most frequently include some type of cap for the flue, many of which feature a mesh or screen for spark control.

PRE-BUILT FIREPLACES

Radiant Fireplaces

Radiant pre-built fireplace units—those that are not designed to circulate air—are manufactured in a similar way to those with circulating capabilities. They lack the grilles and air passages of circulating units, but are heavily insulated so that masonry surroundings are not necessary. Some do circulate air through the unit to help lower temperatures around the firebox.

The units are manufactured, as are their heat-circulating counterparts, of steel. The hearth and the firebox are surfaced with a *refractory* (high temperature) material cast in molds to create a brick pattern. The refractory material provides an excellent surface to assist in the radiation of heat to the room. Various models have available outside combustion air intake kits and gas lighters. The additional flue, spacer kits, flashings, and cap assemblies are matched to the specific unit used, and complete assembly is simple and quick.

Most radiant pre-built units have pre-finished black face surfaces. Some manufacturers offer wood mantels, wood and marble surrounds, and marble hearth extensions (to create the front hearth that extends into the room). These components fit the specific unit and install easily. (See Figure 32.)

The relatively light weight of pre-built units allows their use over existing floors of wood frame construction. The sheer bulk and weight of masonry fireplaces, of course, dictates that provisions be made for structurally carrying their weight to some type of foundation or support system. The masonry units utilize a hearth, again of masonry, which cannot be over a combustible surface. The pre-built units with their insulated multiple-wall construction of sides, back, and bottom and the refractory surfaces permits them to rest on plywood. (Some heat shielding may be required at joints between the unit and the hearth extension, etc.)

Heat-Circulating Fireplaces

Heat-circulating pre-built fireplaces combine the benefits of both radiation and air heating and circulation. They are again of multiple-wall steel construction with refractory linings. They feature air passages between steel walls with inlet and outlet air grilles. These units, through gravity, naturally introduce room air into the unit, and the air is heated as it is directed around the heated firebox and discharged as heated air back into the room through the outlet grilles. This process works well, but it can be further enhanced, if desired, by the inclusion of optional electric fans made specifically for the unit. These fans are hidden, of course, so the unit appears clean, with only the firebox opening and grilles visible. (See Figure 33.)

Heat-circulating pre-built units are matched to multiple-wall and insulated pre-built flues. Some utilize a separate air space in the flue as a means of introducing fresh combustion air from outside the building. Other types of units have available as optional kits a duct system and exterior wall grille for that purpose (frequently with a duct damper controlled at the fireplace). Spacers, firestops, flashings, and caps are matched to these units.

Sizes and styles of pre-built units vary with the different manufacturers, as do the proportions of face openings. Most units have all face materials finished in black. Some units feature trim that resembles brass or chrome. Safety screens are furnished as part of the basic units, and most manufacturers offer optional heat-resistant glass doors. Some manufacturers have designed their units with a raised *ash lip* at the front of the firebox hearth. Other manufacturers promote a "flush" hearth floor, which they contend provides a cleaner appearance and makes ash removal and firebox cleaning easier. (See Figure 34.)

Grates are a standard item with some units, but they may be an optional item with others. The most usual types of grates available are those fabricated (by welding and bending) from round or square steel bars. Most of these are simple, clean-looking, and functional, with no attempt at a decorative effect. At least one manufacturer provides, for some units, the same type of grates, but with higher front legs fabricated to resemble decorative andirons with the appearance of the wrought iron work of earlier times.

Through the years, homeowners have sometimes desired fireplaces that departed from the more traditional "wall" fireplaces. Thus, using masonry in a job-built format, fireplaces have been constructed with open front and back, permitting enjoyment of a single fire in two adjoining rooms. Others opted for a projecting corner fireplace with firebox open on the front and one end. Still others created "peninsula" fireplaces, featuring two open faces and one open end. Prior to the development of glass doors, these configurations were much less efficient than the traditional wall fireplace, and many were prone to downdrafts and smoking.

Pre-built fireplace manufacturers have succeeded in designing successful units of all of these configurations, and through their highly developed fabrication techniques they now provide efficient units of the see-through, projecting corner, and peninsula types. The projecting corner units are available in either left-hand or right-hand styles (corner opening on either the left or the right end). Some units have, as standard equipment, safety fire screens with heat-resistant glass doors as an optional feature. Other units come with glass doors included as a standard item. The materials and methods used in manufacturing these pre-built units conform to those employed in the pre-built "wall" fireplace units.

See-through, projecting corner, and peninsula pre-built fireplace units have optional items available for various models. Depending on the model and manufacturer, grates, fans, outside combustion air kits, gas lighter, and decorative trim kits are available, as are the multiple wall and insulated flue components, spacers, flashings, and flue cap assemblies.

Both common sense and building codes require that a noncombustible front hearth area be created outside of the fireplace. This surface can be job-built or provided by the unit manufacturer with a *hearth extension*, which is available as an option. In either case, such a surface should be provided for all faces of the unit (both sides for the see-through, from an end for the projecting corner, and all three faces for the peninsula type of fireplace).

This chapter will later mention codes and clearances required for fireplaces. Even though pre-built fireplaces are frequently referred to as zero clearance fireplace units, there are minimum clearance requirements, which must be maintained and observed when installing them. Homeowners, do-it-yourselfers, and installers should be in strict compliance with those requirements.

Free-Standing Fireplaces

Free-standing fireplace units are available as pre-built units, and some of those units are produced by the same manufacturers that produce the more standard pre-built units discussed previously. One type of free-standing fireplace unit is rectangular, with the fire visible from all four sides. It is frequently referred to as an island-type fireplace. The end panels are of heat-resistant glass, and it comes with glass doors for the front and back as standard equipment. It has, as part of the basic passage, the necessary kit to provide outside combustion air. The same types of flue and flue accessories as those mentioned previously for the other pre-built units are used. Trim kits and a gas log set are available as options. After installing the unit, it and the flue are covered with facing materials to provide the decorative effect desired by the owner. This unit can be installed at floor level or on a raised hearth platform. In either case, a non-combustible extended hearth surface must surround the unit on all four sides.

Through the years, a variety of free-standing fireplace units has been marketed. Basically, two distinctly different materials have been used in their manufacture. Most prevalent has been the use of steel. The steel units have frequently been based on a conical hood design with a raised steel hearth supported by a short pipe welded to a steel saucer-shaped base. These units utilize a stovepipe type of damper in the flue pipe itself. These hood-type units have either a single face opening, or in the case of the round carousel type, openings all around with multiple glass sides and a glass door. The steel island-type unit features a rectangular or square hood shape and has a raised hearth supported on a single column and base plate. One type of unit is of arch shape with a single glass door for access to the firebox. (See Figure 35.)

In addition to the types of free-standing units fabricated from steel, units have been created from ceramic materials. Such free-standing units are often onion-shaped. The fire clay used for the combustion chamber, or firebox, is similar to the high temperature material used for the interior of kilns and ceramic furnaces. The material is vitrified (or fired) in its manufacture in kilns at a temperature of 2,350 degrees or more. The shape and thermal retention properties of these ceramic units result in a high degree of efficiency and very minimal ash accumulation.

The exterior of a ceramic free-standing fireplace is either a textured, glazed surface or a glazed ceramic mosaic tile surface.

Both are available in a wide range of colors. The units can be provided with multiple-wall steel flues, and utilize an in-flue damper. Glass doors are available either standard or as an option, depending on the manufacturer. The design of many of the units results in exterior surfaces that are safe for children to touch. As with any wood-burning pre-built unit, there are minimum distances that must be maintained between the unit and adjacent walls, etc. They should also be placed on non-combustible "hearth" surfaces.

CODES AND FIREPLACES

Several types of codes apply to the construction, manufacture, and installation of fireplaces. In addition, there are requirements and recommendations of insurance companies, component and unit manufacturers, and lending agencies.

Reliable manufacturers, in their efforts to provide safe components and units, submit their products to various organizations and agencies for testing, evaluation, approval, and certification. These testing and certifying agencies include: U.L. (Underwriters' Laboratories), B.O.C.A. (Building Officials and Code Administrators International, Inc.), S.B.C.C. (Southern Building Code Congress), and the I.C.B.O. (International Conference of Building Officials). In addition, some units are listed with Los Angeles City-Approval Agency, and in Canada, Warnock Hersey International, Inc., certifying to U.L.C. The N.B.C. (National Building Code) requirements concerning fireplaces have been recommended by the National Board of Fire Underwriters. Listing and certification by the entities listed above help assure safety of the fireplace for the homeowner or home buyer.

The F.H.A. (Federal Housing Administration) and the V.A. (Veterans Administration) have requirements that must be met if a home is to be approved for their loans. Some regional or local financial institutions that make home loans may have their own list of requirements addressing fireplace construction.

Individual municipalities have their own building codes. These codes may include detailed code requirements governing fireplace construction, or they may make reference to one or more of the national or international codes. Some cities now ban new fireplace construction, while some others permit new fireplaces while limiting (or scheduling) times when they can be used, based on air pollution conditions at the particular times. In any event, those contemplating construction or installation of a fireplace should check applicable code requirements prior to commencing construction or purchase.

Construction and installation requirements and codes have as their purpose providing safety for the building's inhabitants and ensuring the safe and satisfactory performance of fireplaces. In that context, they should be viewed as a help rather than a hindrance. Typical codes and requirements cover such items as minimum distances of separation between wood framing members and the front, back, and sides of the fireplace; minimum distances to be maintained between wood and the flue; minimum distance of separation of wood trim from the fireplace face opening; and minimum distance to be met, or exceeded, between the top of the fireplace opening and any projecting trim or mantel made of combustible material.

Firestops are usually required at any point where chimneys or flues pass through floors, ceiling, and roof decking, or roof sheathing. These firestops must be of non-combustible material, and are now mainly sheet metal. These flat, plate-type units have a hole in the center for the flue and extend past the framing surrounding the larger opening through which the flue passes. They can serve as the required spacer to ensure the necessary clearance between flue and wood framing, and they can serve the firestop function as well. The firestops are installed on the bottom of floor joists if the flue pipe passes through a framed opening between floors, and are placed on the top of the ceiling joists when the pipe passes through the ceiling and into the attic space.

Pre-built fireplace units have minimum clearance requirements from any combustible materials, and the difference in manufacturers and their different designs results in clearances appropriate for each specific unit. One manufacturer has various units that result in three different sets of requirements. The distances to be maintained between the unit and any combustible materials at the back and sides are listed as ½ inch, 1 inch, and 2 inches, depending on the unit. All of their units require ½ inch between the side of the unit at the front and the vertical wood studs that frame the wall opening. All of their units can be placed directly on top of combustible floor materials (plywood, wood flooring, etc.). Some manufacturers require that the space around their units contain non-combustible insulation.

The manufacturer used here as the example requires that any wall intersecting the fireplace wall be a minimum distance from the fireplace opening of 12 inches, 12½ inches, or 20 inches, depending on which unit is being installed. This particular manufacturer lists a minimum of two inches clear space around their flue pipe for all of their units. The fireplace unit requires that a sheet metal safety strip be placed under the front of the unit and extend out onto the floor surface. This unit-wide three-inch strip is to extend 1½ inches under the unit, leaving 1½ inches projecting outside of the unit face.

Restrictions for the distance from the edges of the actual firebox opening to any combustible face material for different units are 9 inches, 10 $\frac{5}{8}$ inches, or 12 inches. Projecting mantels or combustible materials must be placed a safe distance above the top of the firebox opening. As an example, varying with different models, a 5-inch projection requires a vertical clearance of 9, 10, or 12 inches. A projecting mantel requires a vertical distance of 17, 18, or 19 inches.

Clear, illustrated installation instructions accompany each pre-built fireplace unit. They give the actual clearance requirements for that specific unit. The instructions are extremely important and should be carefully observed. All units require a non-combustible hearth in front of the entire unit and extending past the sides of the unit. This surface may be created with the optional pre-finished "hearth extension" available from the manufacturer, or may be job-built of non-combustible materials such as slate, ceramic or quarry tiles, brick, etc. Minimum hearth dimensions are given in the installation instructions.

FIREPLACE ACCESSORIES

A wide variety of fireplace accessories is available, in a large selection of different styles. The various accessories include, but are not limited to, cranes (for cooking), grates, andirons, screens, glass doors, bellows, fire tool sets, gas lighters, gas log sets, and flue-cleaning tools.

Cranes and Grates

Cranes, of course, are the pivoting arms that can be positioned over the fire so that cooking vessels can be hung from them. They are attached to the side of the firebox and are available in several styles and designs.

Grates provide the actual support for the logs in the fireplace and are manufactured of steel or cast iron. Their designs range from simple rod assemblies and simple basket-type cast iron units to more elaborate configurations. (See Figure 36.)

Andirons and Screens

Andirons can be purchased in a wide array of styles and materials. Andirons are now predominantly intended for decorative purposes and are not a necessary device to the actual function of the fireplace.

Screens provide protection from sparks and embers entering the room from the firebox. Again, many styles are available. Some screens are simply free-standing devices with rigid frames, which stand against and in front of the firebox opening. These screens may be one-piece designs, or they may be manufactured with a large center panel and two smaller end panels that are hinged from the main panel. Some screens work on a "drapery" principle and can be pulled to each side of the opening. They are available as either a surface-mounted unit or a unit that mounts just inside of the front face of the firebox opening. (See Figure 37.)

Glass Doors

Glass doors are produced in many different designs and configurations. Using heat-resistant glass, they provide total containment of the fire while permitting an open view of it. As with screens, they may be of the surface-mount variety, or actually install just inside of the firebox opening. Most door units are available as either a pair of doors, hinged at the outsides of the unit, or as four doors operating in a bi-fold format. Trim for glass door units can be simple or elaborate, and manufacturers produce door units trimmed in brass, bronze, chrome, or black. (See Figure 38.)

Fire Tool Sets

The selection of fire tool sets available is almost mind-boggling. Sets are available that hang from brackets attached to the fireplace face or that have their own free-standing "stand," which permits positioning them anywhere on the hearth. Designs vary and include Modern, Early American, Classic, Western, Southwest, Colonial, etc. Although the tools themselves are of steel, the handles are available in wood, brass, bronze, steel, enameled steel, and leather. Most sets available include poker, shovel, and broom. Log tongs are also available. Log baskets are sometimes available with trim to match the fire tool sets. Homeowners should have little trouble obtaining fireplace accessories that match their tastes and decorating themes.

FIREWOOD SELECTION

There is an old saying regarding wood-burning fireplace owners that firewood heats you three times: once when you cut it, once when you stack it, and once when you burn it. There is probably more than a little truth to that observation, as can be attested to by anyone who has worked up a sweat cutting, splitting, and stacking firewood. Some homeowners live in wooded areas where their firewood is literally there for the taking. Others may have to rely on firewood providers and purchase their firewood on either a delivered or a haul-it-yourself basis. Some suppliers offer firewood in either split or unsplit condition, leaving it up to the purchasers to decide if they want to split the larger chunks themselves.

Firewood is usually priced, sold, and delivered on the standard measure of the *cord*. The term refers to a stack of firewood with an overall volume of 128 cubic feet. The accepted standard cord measures 8 feet in length, 4 feet wide, and 4 feet high. Although the overall volume totals 128 cubic feet, there may be as much as 30 cubic feet or more of the volume made up of air spaces between the logs. The logs may be of any length as long as the total volume is 128 cubic feet when stacked. Logically enough, wood that has been split will stack tighter than whole logs, and a cord of split wood should contain more wood than one of unsplit logs. A standard cord may contain anywhere from 60 to 110 cubic feet of solid wood. Certainly the firewood seller has considerably more labor in the cord of split wood, and the cord price will reflect that. (See Figure 39.)

Another smaller quantity of firewood is frequently sold as a *face cord* or *short cord*. It conforms to the 8-foot length and 4-foot height of the cord, but the log length (the stack width) can vary. Most often the width of the face cord is 16 inches, 20 inches, or 24 inches. Again, the face or short cord can be of whole logs or split logs. The homeowner purchasing a face cord should try to buy lengths that will properly fit his fireplace without additional cutting. (See Figure 40.)

Some wood suppliers sell their firewood by weight or truckload, and, of course, the amount of wood obtained from either of these methods varies with the species of the wood, the amount of moisture in the wood, and the size of the truck. A full cord of well-seasoned hardwood generally weighs from 2,500 to 3,000 pounds, according to the species. If the hardwood is "green," the same cord can weigh more than two tons.

The amount of heating potential, or heat value, of firewood varies dramatically with the amount of moisture it contains. Green, or just cut, firewood contains a large amount of moisture. Kiln- or oven-dried wood can have all moisture removed, but the drying process is too expensive for firewood and is limited to producing finished lumber for the construction and furniture industries. Air-dried firewood is the most logical and productive choice for providing heat. The table below lists a range of moisture contents and their effect on the percentage of usable heat the wood in those conditions can be expected to provide.

PERCENT OF MOISTURE CONTAINED	PERCENT OF ESTIMATED USABLE HEAT
0 (oven- or kiln-dried)	103.4
10	101.6
20 (hardwood, air-dried)	100.00
40	96.5
80	89.7
100	85.0

Since green firewood, or firewood with a high moisture content, burns less efficiently and provides less heating value, it should be purchased at lower prices than air-dried and seasoned firewood. If such green wood is purchased early in the spring and stacked properly, it will have sufficient time to season and air-dry so that it is satisfactory for use during the following heating season. Ideally, it takes from six to twelve months for green wood to season to the lowest moisture level for air-dried firewood. A quick way to make an educated guess at whether firewood is seasoned or not is to inspect the ends of the pieces visually, and to peel the bark from some sample pieces from the middle of the pile. The ends should have checks, or small cracks, radiating outward from the center, or heartwood. After peeling the bark from the sample pieces, the exposed wood should be dry to the touch.

The burning characteristics of wood vary with the species.

Elm burns fairly slowly, while pine and white birch burn much more quickly, producing crackling and frequent sparks. Generally, soft woods are easier and quicker to light than are the hardwood species.

Heat values of various species are generally dependent on the density or weight of the wood. It follows that heavier wood provides the higher heat values. To give some point of reference to the heating potential of a cord of air-dried native hardwoods such as oak or hickory, that cord of firewood can provide the same heating potential as 130 gallons of No. 2 fuel oil. Heating values of various materials are generally listed in terms of B.T.U.'s (British Thermal Units). A B.T.U. is defined as the amount of heat required to raise the temperature of one pound of water one degree Fahrenheit. The chart below lists several wood species, the weight of an air-dried cord of those species, and the amount of available heat in those cords, expressed in terms of millions of B.T.U.'s. Charts are available that list numerous other species; the species referenced here are provided to illustrate simply the wide difference among the species.

WOOD SPECIES	WEIGHT OF AIR-DRIED CORD (In Pounds)	AVAILABLE HEAT (Millions of B.T.U.'s)
Eastern White Pine	2,080	13.3
Aspen	2,160	12.5
American Elm	2,900	17.2
Red Maple	3,200	18.6
Ash	3,440	20.01
Sugar Maple	3,680	21.3
Red Oak	3,680	21.3
Yellow Birch	3,680	21.3
American Beech	3,760	21.8
White Oak	3,920	24.6
Shagbark Hickory	4,240	24.6

Some firewood dealers may sell cords or loads of individual species. Others may sell cords of "mixed," or "mixed hardwoods." A cord of dense hardwood may provide more heat value, but a mixed cord of hardwood (usually available at a lower price) may offer more heating value per dollar spent. Homeowners in locations with lumbering and sawmills may be able to purchase slabs and mill ends created in the process of squaring up logs for lumber purposes. These configurations have the same heat values as their full-log relatives and can often be purchased at a much lower rate. They may, however, require the buyers to do their own hauling, cutting, and seasoning.

Unburned gases that are present in wood smoke form creosote when they condense on cooler surfaces. Thus creosote is continually formed during the process of the fire burning. It can build up on the interior of the fireplace, the damper assembly, and the interior of the flue. Much has been written about the effects of creosote build-up, its effect on fireplace efficiency and operation, and the potential hazards it may create. Ways to limit the degree of creosote build-up have been frequently discussed, Certainly the new multiple wall and insulated flue systems, with their extremely smooth interior surfaces, and the better draft achieved with today's fireplace units are helpful in this regard. Hotter fires produce less creosote than do slowly burning or smoldering fires. Also, dry hardwoods produce less creosote than do softwoods and wood with a high moisture content. Probably the most important aspects of controlling creosote build-up are checking the flue periodically and cleaning it, or hiring a chimney sweep to clean it for you, to remove the creosote that has collected.

Figure 28. Conventional job-built radiant fireplaces.

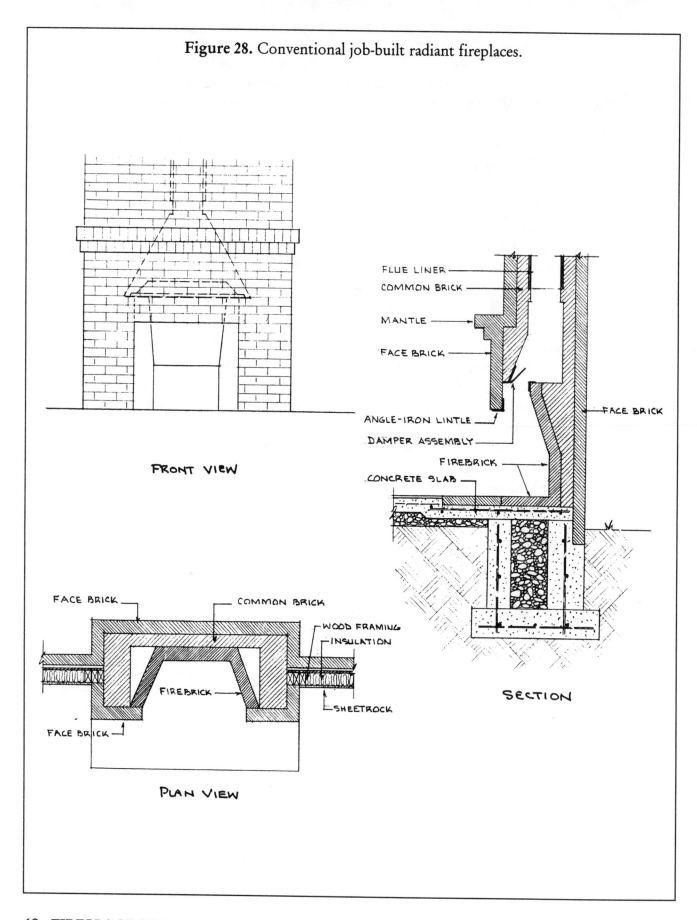

FRONT VIEW

FLUE LINER
COMMON BRICK
MANTLE
FACE BRICK
ANGLE-IRON LINTLE
DAMPER ASSEMBLY
FIREBRICK
CONCRETE SLAB
FACE BRICK

SECTION

FACE BRICK
COMMON BRICK
WOOD FRAMING
INSULATION
FIREBRICK
SHEETROCK
FACE BRICK

PLAN VIEW

Figure 29. Basic masonry fireplace dimensions.
(All dimensions are in inches.)

Range of Face Opening Dimensions		Range of Depth of Firebox (Thickness of face material not included)	Nominal Flue Size
Width	Height		
24	24 to 28	16	8 x 12
26	24 to 28	16	8 x 12
28	24 to 28	16	8 x 12
30	29 to 30	16	12 x 12
32	29 to 30	16	12 x 12
34	29 to 30	16	12 x 12
36	29 to 31	16 to 18	12 x 12
38	30 to 31	16 to 18	12 x 12
40	29 to 31	16 to 18	12 x 16
42	31 to 32	16 to 18	16 x 16
44	31 to 32	16 to 18	16 x 16
46	31 to 32	16 to 18	16 x 16
48	32	18 to 20	16 x 16
50	32 to 34	18 to 20	16 x 16
52	32 to 34	18 to 20	16 x 16
54	34 to 37	20	16 x 16
56	36 to 37	20	16 x 16
60	36 to 40	22	16 x 20
72	39 to 40	22 to 24	20 x 20
84	40	24	20 x 20
96	40	24	20 x 20

Figure 30. Double-walled steel heat-circulating fireplace.

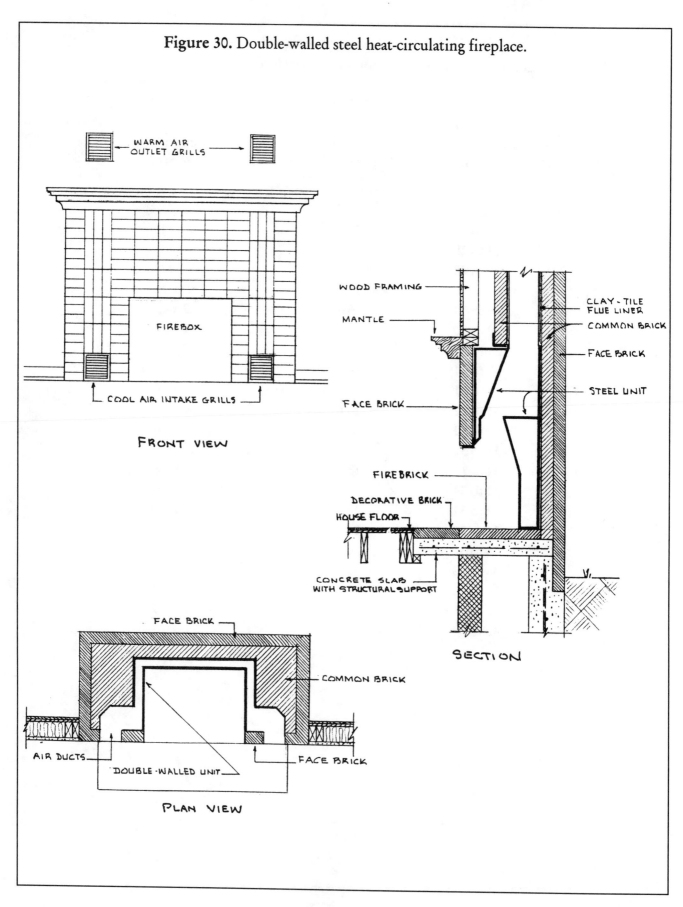

Figure 31. Basic heat-circulating fireplace dimensions.
(All dimensions are in inches.)

Range of Face Opening Dimensions		Range of Depth of Firebox (Thickness of face material not included)	Nominal Flue Size
Width	Height		
28	22	15	12 x 12
32	24	16	12 x 12
33	27½	16	12 x 12
33½	27	16³/₄	12 x 12
36	25	17	12 x 16
37	25 to 27½	16	12 x 12 to 12 x 16
38	29½	17³/₄	12 x 16
40	30½	17	12 x 16
41	30¹/₈	18	12 x 16
42	32	19	16 x 16
46	29	18	16 x 20
49	30¹/₈	18	16 x 20
50	34	20	16 x 20
54	31	19	16 x 20

Figure 32. Pre-built radiant fireplace.

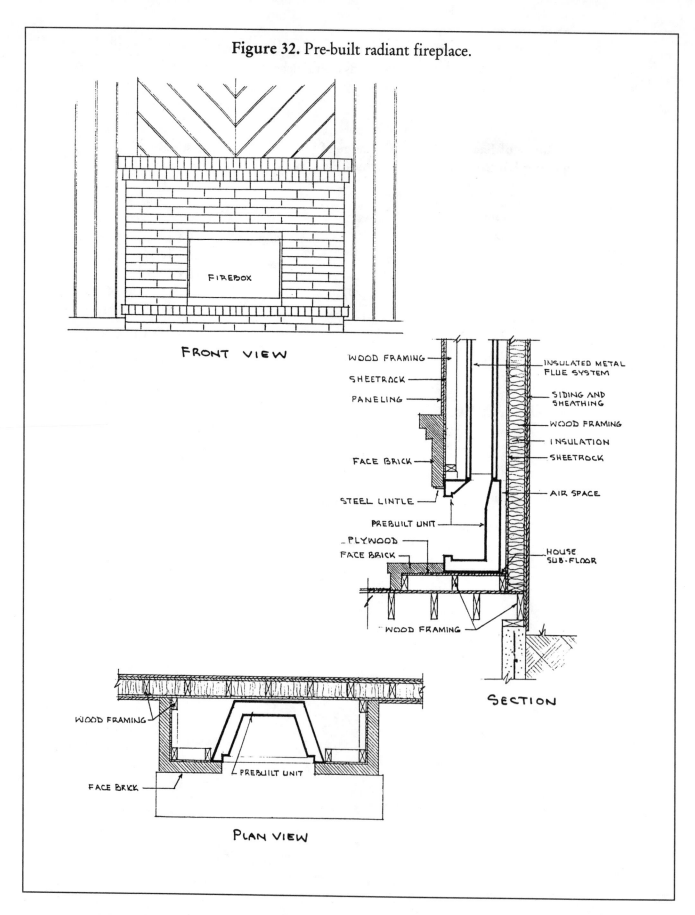

FRONT VIEW

FIREBOX

WOOD FRAMING

SHEETROCK

PANELING

FACE BRICK

STEEL LINTLE

PREBUILT UNIT

PLYWOOD

FACE BRICK

WOOD FRAMING

INSULATED METAL FLUE SYSTEM

SIDING AND SHEATHING

WOOD FRAMING

INSULATION

SHEETROCK

AIR SPACE

HOUSE SUB-FLOOR

SECTION

WOOD FRAMING

FACE BRICK

PREBUILT UNIT

PLAN VIEW

Figure 33. Pre-built heat-circulating fireplace.

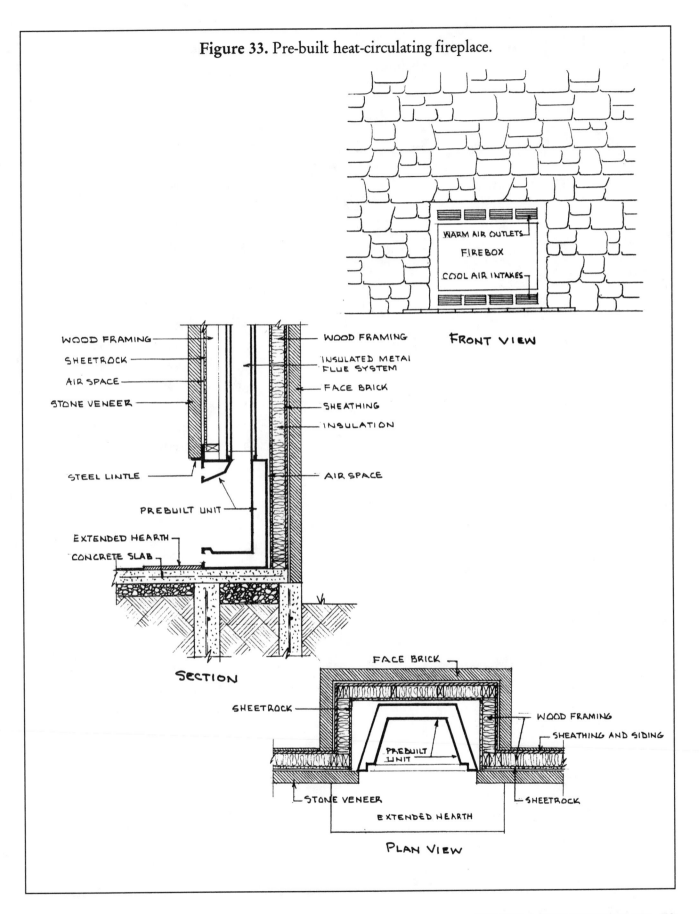

WARM AIR OUTLETS

FIREBOX

COOL AIR INTAKES

FRONT VIEW

WOOD FRAMING

SHEETROCK

AIR SPACE

STONE VENEER

STEEL LINTLE

PREBUILT UNIT

EXTENDED HEARTH

CONCRETE SLAB

WOOD FRAMING

INSULATED METAL FLUE SYSTEM

FACE BRICK

SHEATHING

INSULATION

AIR SPACE

SECTION

FACE BRICK

SHEETROCK

WOOD FRAMING

SHEATHING AND SIDING

PREBUILT UNIT

STONE VENEER

SHEETROCK

EXTENDED HEARTH

PLAN VIEW

Figure 34. Range of typical dimensions of zero-clearance units.
(All dimensions are in inches.)

Face Opening Dimensions		Inside Depth of Firebox	Overall Unit Dimensions		
Width	Height		Width	Height	Depth
36	21½	16½	41	35	22
36	20½	17	43	33½	23½
36	21	17	43	38 $1/8$	23
36	21	17½	46	46	24
36	21	15	40	37	20
36	20	15½	40	32	21
36	22	16½	42	37½	23
41	23	21½	46½	39½	23
41	22	16½	47	38	22
41	23	18	45½	39	24
42	21	19½	52	47	24
42	21	18	49	39	23
42	20½	18	49	33½	23

Figure 35. Free-standing fireplace units.

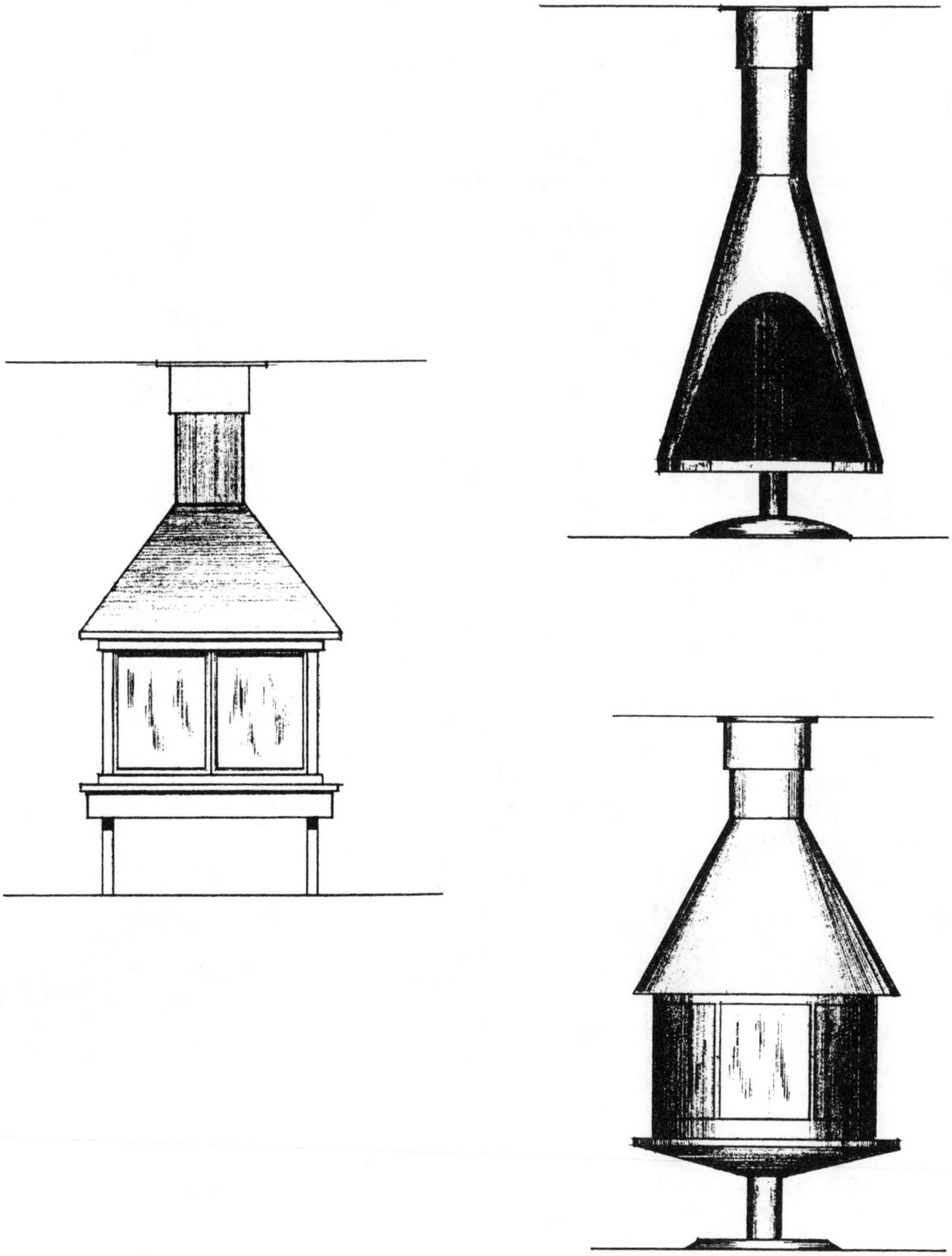

Figure 36. Cranes and grates.

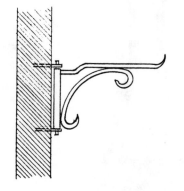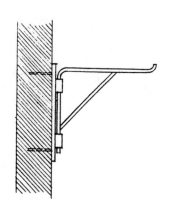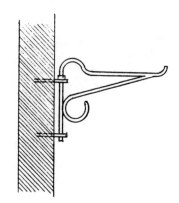

PIVOTING STEEL COOKING CRANES

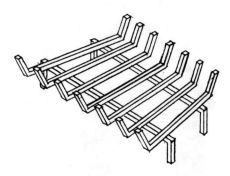

WELDED STEEL GRATE

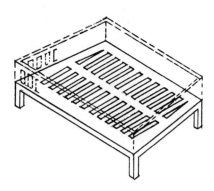

CAST-IRON GRATE

Figure 37. Types of fireplace safety screens.

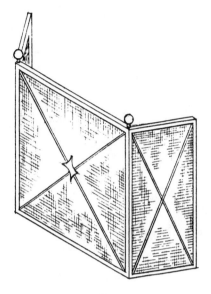

HINGED THREE PANEL

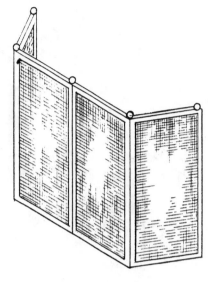

HINGED FOUR PANEL

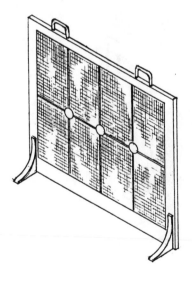

ONE PIECE

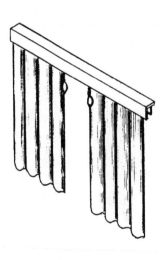

DRAPERY-TYPE

Figure 38. Types of glass doors for fireplaces.

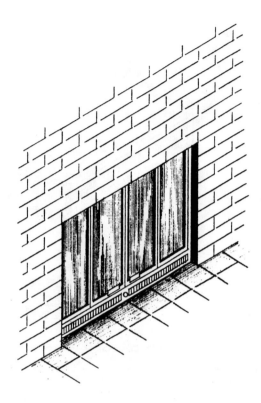

INSIDE-OF-OPENING MOUNT

EXTERIOR SURFACE MOUNT

Figure 39. Standard cord and face cord firewood measure.

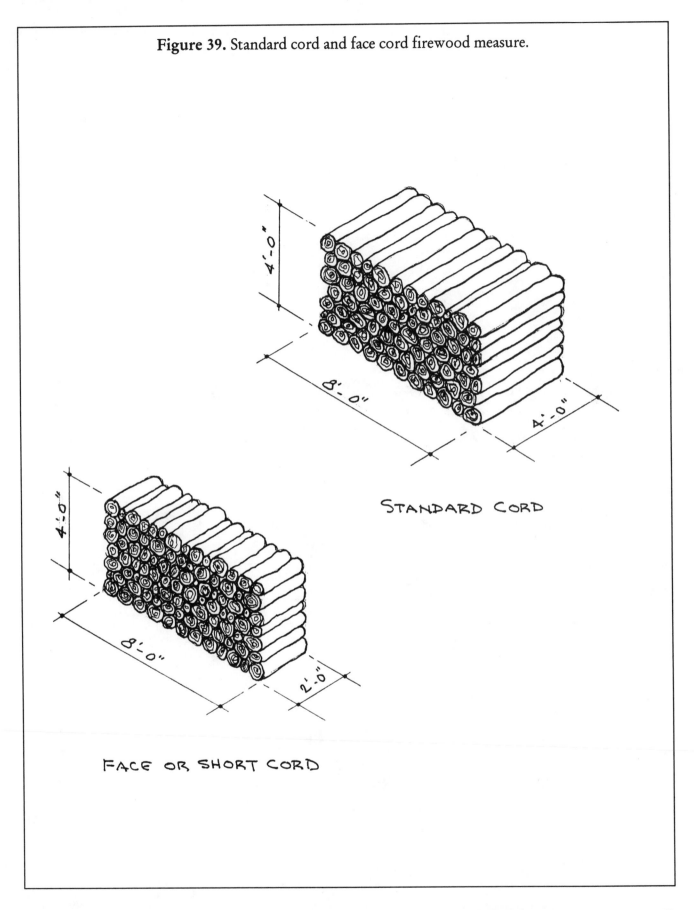

4'-0"

8'-0"

4'-0"

STANDARD CORD

4'-0"

8'-0"

2'-0"

FACE OR SHORT CORD

Chapter 4

Fireplace Designs

The purpose of this chapter is to provide a variety of fireplace designs of various basic styles. These designs may be used to create fireplaces in new or existing homes, offices, and commercial buildings. They are also intended to provide ideas the readers can incorporate in their own creative fireplace designs.

The designs are basically presented in the format of the styles in which they have their origins. Each design has a brief description of the finish materials used in its construction. The reader is cautioned that it is imperative any fireplace design be analyzed in regard to its conforming to locally applicable codes and restrictions prior to commencing actual construction. In essence, the designs are intended as ideas for the visual aspects of fireplaces. Most of the designs can be adapted to permit their creation with job-built conventional or heat-circulating fireplace formats, or with pre-built zero clearance fireplace units.

Each design is briefly described as to the materials it incorporates. Many of the designs could be based on materials other than those shown. Not everyone may agree that the names chosen for the categorization of styles are proper and correct. They were simply chosen as a way of categorizing the designs as to the feelings they convey.

Figure 40. English-style fireplace design.

$\mathcal{B}$ased on a pre-built heat-circulating unit, this design features a minimum of brickwork at the sides of the firebox, a massive wood header above the fireplace unit, and rustic wood trim defining inset panels of stucco or plaster (drywall could be used also).

Figure 41. English-style fireplace design.

This design uses a conventional fireplace format. The firebox opening is trimmed with brick (including the brick arch above the opening), and the face is brick up to the height of the wood mantel. The plaster or drywall surface above the mantel slopes back and upward, creating a hood-like shape.

Figure 42. Italian-style fireplace design.

A conventional job-built fireplace, this design uses brick for the entire face. The firebox opening is topped with an arch of bricks of tapering heights, and the two inset niches balance the large area of brick.

Figure 43. Italian-style fireplace design.

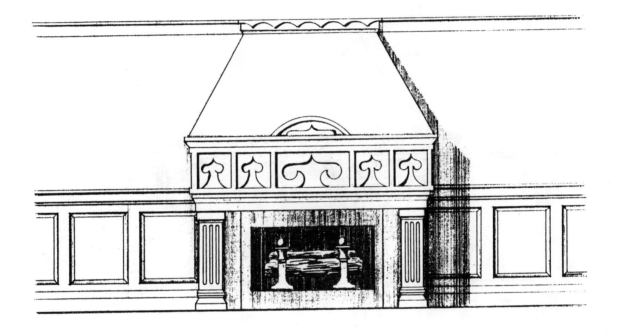

*S*hown with a pre-built radiant unit, the massive hooded shape above can be made up
of cast plaster components or wood, or could be formed of drywall and
finally stuccoed. The columns at the front of the fireplace are of wood,
as is the paneled wall wainscot.

Figure 44. Dutch-style fireplace design.

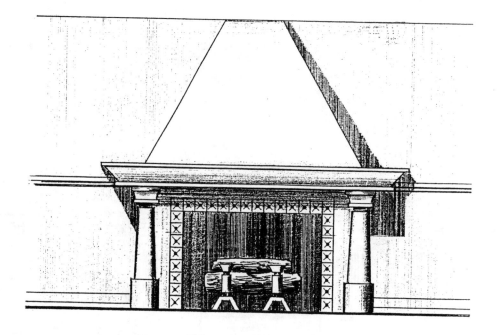

*D*ecorative glazed tile surrounds the firebox opening of this conventionally constructed fireplace. Two thick tapered wood columns support the massive wood mantel. The hood-shaped area above, of drywall or plaster, slopes upward and back from the mantel. The wall surface, again of drywall or plaster, is broken only by the wood base and horizontal wood trim installed in line with the bottom of the mantel.

Figure 45. French-style fireplace design.

Two tall wood columns flank each side of the fireplace in this design. The marble surround frames the conventional masonry firebox. The fireplace is further defined with heavy wood square columns and mantel. The area directly above the mantel is of mirrors installed in individual tile-like fashion. Heavy wood trim frames the sides and top of the mirrored area.

Figure 46. Spanish-style fireplace design.

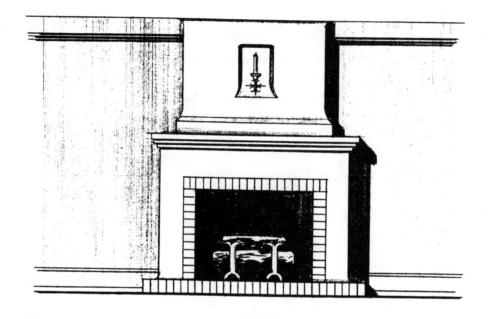

The conventional firebox opening is surrounded by brick. The balance of the fireplace face is of plaster (or drywall) with a simple wood mantel separating the wider, deeper bottom portion from the narrower, shallower upper portion. A slightly indented area in the center provides a natural spot for mounting a candelabra or other decorative item.

Figure 47. Spanish-style fireplace design.

The simply-shaped projecting face of this fireplace is composed of drywall or plaster. A raised brick hearth supports the tapered wood columns with their wood corbels and connecting beam. Brick provides the surround at the firebox. Hanging light fixtures and a centerpiece of wrought iron finish the fireplace.

Figure 48. Colonial-style fireplace design.

A conventional fireplace, this design surrounds the firebox with marble or painted metal. The surround is framed sides and top with wood. The wood mantel and chair rail atop the wood wainscot incorporate a design with origins in the Greek-key design. Wood ceiling and base trim complete the design.

Figure 49. Colonial-style fireplace design.

The shallow projecting back portion and the deeper projecting front portion of this fireplace including the mantel are of hardwood (or hardwood plywood). The actual firebox surround is of brick. Ceiling cove mold and fancy base trim finish the desired effect.

Figure 50. Colonial-style fireplace design.

The fireplace in this design has its face flush with the room wall. The firebox is surrounded with marble or thin cut stone. The balance of the design is made up of the hardwood inset-panel wall treatment.

Figure 51. Colonial-style fireplace design.

A very simple projecting wood face and mantel define the fireplace, which has a firebox surround of marble. Deep ceiling and base cove trim finish the wall of wide vertical wood paneling.

Figure 52. Colonial-style fireplace design.

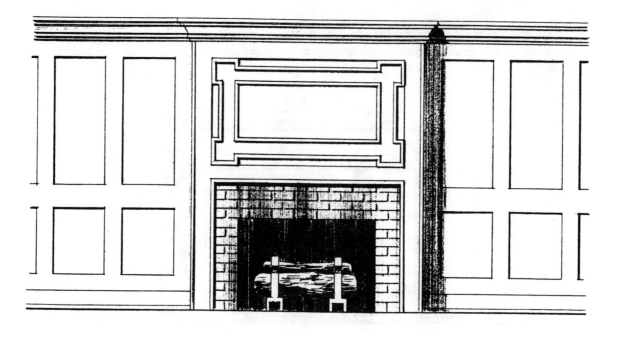

$\mathscr{B}$rick surrounds the firebox of the conventional projecting fireplace. The balance of the fireplace is covered with hardwood, including the inset panel with the design-created wood molding. The wood wall surfaces include inset panels, and wood ceiling and base trim complete the design.

Figure 53. Colonial-style fireplace design.

𝒯he conventional firebox has a surround of either painted metal or marble. The fireplace from mantel down is faced with wood and features a horizontal band of fancy wood molding, which can be either vertically grooved or fluted. Additional wood is incorporated for ceiling and base trim. The wood in this design is intended to be painted.

Figure 54. Colonial-style fireplace design.

M̶arble surrounds the firebox in this design. The entire face of the fireplace is wood, with the mantel and design above it formed with wood moldings attached to that surface. A wainscot of matching wood completes the design. It is suggested that all wood surfaces be painted rather than stained or varnished.

Figure 55. Colonial-style fireplace design.

The wide projecting fireplace has its corners defined by tall rectangular wood columns. The fireplace face is covered with wood, and the upper panel created with wood molding. Stepped moldings frame the marble or cut stone surround of the firebox. Wall surfaces are composed of wood in an inset panel design. This design could be finished in either stained or painted wood.

Figure 56. Early American fireplace design.

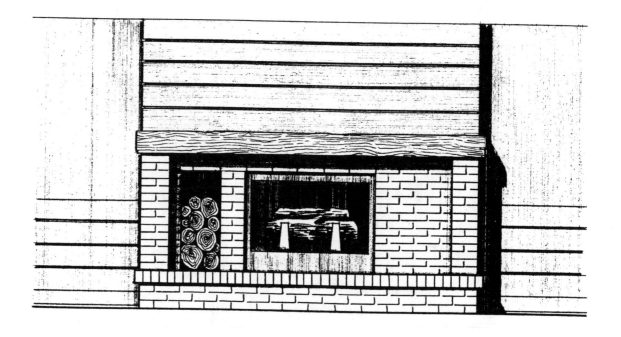

This massive fireplace is based on a pre-built fireplace unit, which sits on a raised brick hearth. Brick makes up the entire lower portion of the fireplace, which has an open wood storage area. A heavy rough-timber mantel is supported on the projecting brick at each end of the fireplace. Thick horizontal wood planking covers the upper face and is used as a wall wainscot as well.

Figure 57. Early American fireplace design.

A broad wood cove molding frames the brickwork of this flush-with-the-wall fireplace. The firebox and a display niche (resembling an early oven) have arched brick above them. The recess below the display niche is for the storage of firewood. Wide individual planks are used for the vertical wall paneling.

Figure 58. Early American fireplace design.

The stair-step effect of the brick at the right side of the fireplace and the back of the brick seating area keep this all-brick design from being harsh in appearance. A pre-built heat-circulating unit is used, so no additional surround is necessary. The recess beneath the seating area provides storage for firewood. The wall can either be papered with a vertical pattern, or paneled with car-siding or board-and-bead siding.

Figure 59. Early American fireplace design.

Stone is used for faces, hearth, and mantel for this projecting conventional fireplace. A recessed niche above the mantel provides a spot to display some favorite possession. The fireplace is flanked by cabinets and bookshelves of painted wood.

Figure 60. Country-style fireplace design.

A brick wainscot frames the flush pre-built heat-circulating unit. Vertical planks with angle braces extend to the horizontal plank at the top of the wall, and thinner wood planks cap the brick wainscot. A large quilt block is prominently displayed on the drywall or plaster wall surface to provide the finishing touch.

Figure 61. Country-style fireplace design.

This extremely simple design surrounds the pre-built heat-circulating unit with native stone. The balance of the fireplace is covered with wood, capped with a simple wood mantel. Random width wall paneling completes the design.

Figure 62. Country-style fireplace design.

The pre-built heat-circulating unit is surrounded with brick, including the raised brick hearth. The balance of the design is wood, including the mantel. The face of the wood front is highlighted by the carved or painted wheat motif.

Figure 63. Country-style fireplace design.

*N*ative field stone, or rubble stone, creates the face of this fireplace with its pre-built radiant unit. A thick wood mantel caps the stonework. The fireplace is contained between the two cabinets created with vertical one-inch boards. The cabinets are purposely kept shorter than ceiling height to permit displaying favorite items on top.

Figure 64. Country-style fireplace design.

Brick creates this entire design with the exception of the high wood shelf with its wood bracket supports. The center, lower portion of the fireplace is recessed eight inches, and it contains the conventional firebox with recesses for display and storage of firewood. The brick surface becomes a pleasant backdrop for fire tools and bellows.

Figure 65. Country-style fireplace design.

The conventional firebox is flush with the wall and has an arched brick surround. The arch of the brick is echoed in the two-layer wood face adjacent to it. The wood molding frames the wood face. The wall surface features horizontal and vertical boards, which form inset panel areas. The inset panels can be wood or painted drywall, or have wallpaper or vinyl wall covering.

Figure 66. Country-style fireplace design.

This fireplace is kept simple so that it becomes a natural spot to display interesting items. The pre-built heat-circulating unit is surrounded with brick. The top courses of brick are laid "flat" and stepped out to support the brick mantel, which caps the whole assembly.

Figure 67. Country-style fireplace design.

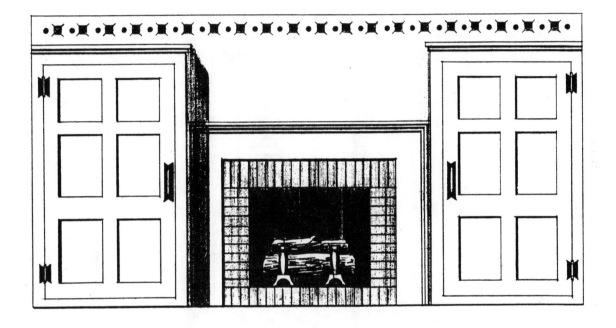

A recessed contemporary fireplace and two simple projecting cabinets form the basis of this design. The firebox is raised and surrounded with brick. A clean wood surface surrounds the brick and is framed with a wood molding. The cabinets have inset panel doors and wrought iron-style hardware. The final design element is the stenciled painted border just below the ceiling.

Figure 68. Rustic fireplace design.

$\mathcal{H}$eavy rustic wood frames this fireplace and creates the mantel. The face of the conventional fireplace is brick, and the projecting brick at each side of the firebox continues to ceiling height as strong vertical design elements. The rustic effect is heightened with vertical wall paneling.

Figure 69. Rustic fireplace design.

Thick wood frames the fireplace, bookshelves, and log storage recesses. A wide, heavy piece of rough-dressed timber creates the mantel spanning the whole assembly. The face of the conventional fireplace is of brick, purposely devoid of projections or decorative patterns.

Figure 70. Rustic fireplace design.

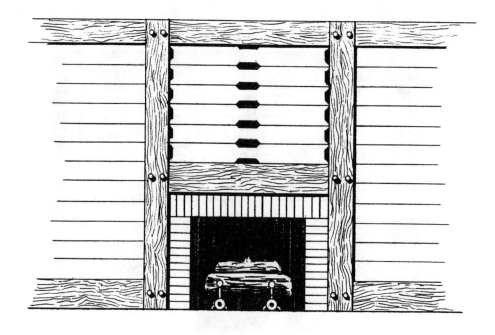

The only brick exposed in this conventional fireplace is that surrounding the firebox. Ceiling trim, base trim, and the fireplace make use of wide wood planks. Projecting wood dowels accent the intersections of the planks. Horizontal boards serve as wall paneling and the upper face of the fireplace. Those on the fireplace have notches to provide additional interest.

Figure 71. Rustic fireplace design.

Irregular stone is featured in this conventional fireplace. A heavy rustic wood mantel provides a strong horizontal accent. The shape of the fireplace is made more interesting by tapering the sides of portions of the stone face. Wood wall paneling provides an appropriate background for the stonework.

Figure 72. Southwest-style fireplace design.

Cut stone and wood create the face of this fireplace with its pre-built heat-circulating unit. Angular lines create the arch effect. The hearth is raised and extends the full width of the fireplace. The area above the wood mantel is made up of wood planks, spaced apart, which form a triangular pattern.

Figure 73. Southwest-style fireplace design.

This design, utilizing a pre-built heat-circulating unit, has a strong central point of interest in the arch with its inset panel of sheet copper. The copper can either be kept polished or allowed to oxidize and reach its natural patina. Rather than a typical mantel, there are two wood mantel sections, one on each side of the arch, with projecting wood corbel brackets.

Figure 74. Southwest-style fireplace design.

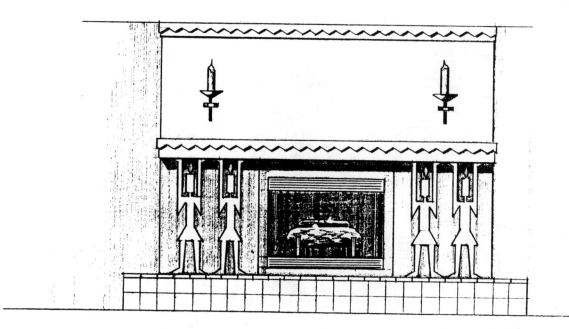

Quarry tile provides the finished surfaces of the long raised hearth. The entire face of the fireplace is of stucco, plaster, or textured drywall. Mantel face and top trim are created by applying one plain board to the surface, and overlaying it with a narrower board cut with a triangular pattern. Simplified figures are cut (two to four inches thick) and appear to be supporting the mantel. The figures, though simplified, resemble Navajo "Yei" figures.

Figure 75. Southwest-style fireplace design.

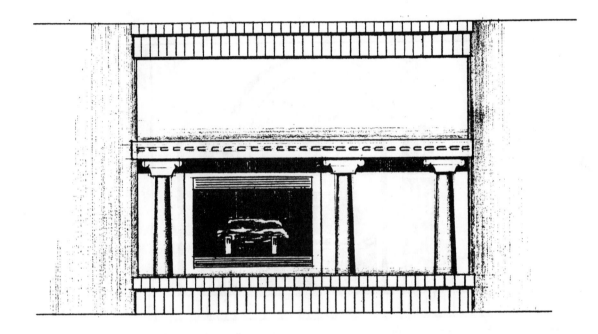

The only visible brick in this design creates the raised hearth and becomes the trim at the top of the fireplace face. The face of the fireplace can be drywall, plaster, or stucco. Tapered wood columns with simple wood capitals support a heavy wood mantel, which is enlivened with a line of simple gouge, or "finger groove," carving.

Figure 76. Southwest-style fireplace design.

Brick defines the raised hearth and contrasts with the plaster or stucco fireplace face. Projecting arches frame shelves and firebox. The center arch is highlighted with a piece of artwork, or as shown here, wrought iron in a Southwest motif.

Figure 77. Southwest-style fireplace design.

This design relies solely on stucco or plaster with the exclusion of the four simple round wood columns. The mantel and arch area projects from the fireplace face as does the raised hearth. The arch interior features a three-dimensional sculpted design (applied to the fireplace and then coated with plaster or stucco).

Figure 78. Southwest-style fireplace design.

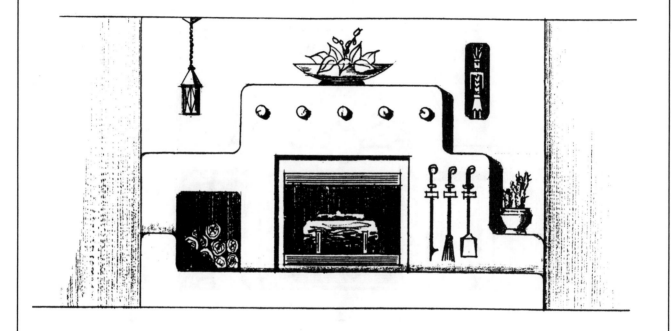

Echoing shapes of the Pueblos, this design is based on stucco as the sole finish material. The raised hearth has a small raised end adjacent to the log storage niche. Rather than a mantel, the lower face of the fireplace projects ten to twelve inches from the face above it, providing "mantel space" in a little different way. Projecting small peeled wood logs evoke the feelings of the vigas (support beams of adobe houses) of buildings of the Southwest.

Figure 79. Southwest-style fireplace design.

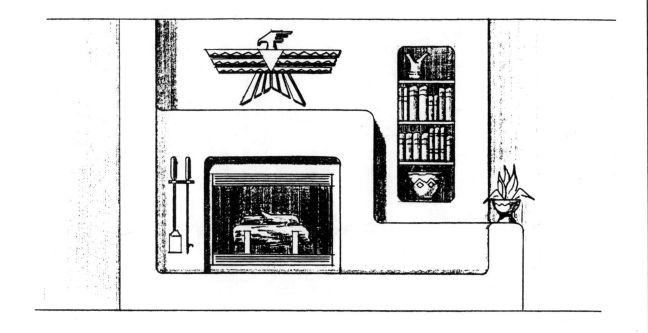

$\mathcal{P}$rojecting from the wall in three different layers, this stucco fireplace has a different look. The large niche in the right side of the face provides a place for books and collected treasures.

Figure 80. Southwest-style fireplace design.

*S*tucco comprises the entire fireplace face, with the arches built up prior to finish stuccoing. The raised hearth is constructed of brick. The plain surfaces of stucco become ideal for attaching candelabra and fire tools, and the hearth is a fine place to display Indian pottery or baskets.

Figure 81. Southwest-style fireplace design.

Only stucco is used in this simple design. The projecting arch flows into short "wing walls" at its two sides. The raised hearth extends in front of the wing walls. Curved corners impart a fluid effect to the design. The sculpted panel inside the arch could be cast, built up, and stuccoed, or carved in wood.

Figure 82. Southwest-style fireplace design.

Slopes and curves give this design a different look. Kept simple through the use of only stucco as the finish material, it provides a backdrop for display. The recessed niche echoes the shape of the projecting stucco surfaces below. Ends of the raised hearth angle back to the wall at forty-five degrees.

Figure 83. Southwest-style fireplace design.

*S*tucco finish, softened with curved corners, is the basis of this design. The face surrounding the firebox and the wood storage niche project from the back face some eight to ten inches to create a mantel surface. The raised hearth projects another sixteen to eighteen inches. The log niche is echoed in the smaller display niche above it.

Figure 84. Contemporary fireplace design.

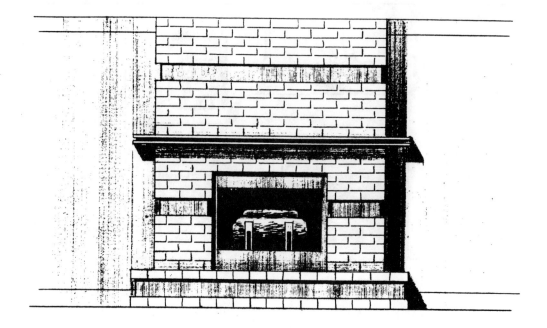

$\mathcal{S}$imple brick surfaces and strong horizontal bands of inset copper, marble, or painted steel give this design a crisp look. Even the raised brick hearth has an inset band to echo those above. The mantel, of steel, wood, or copper, has a recess in its face to complement the balance of the design.

Figure 85. Contemporary fireplace design.

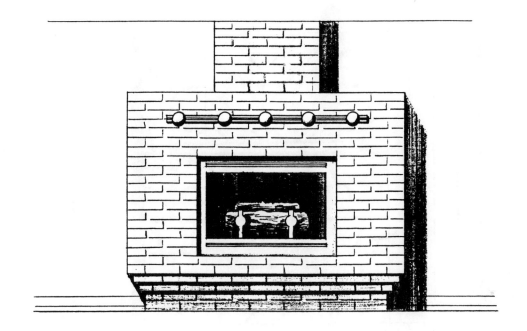

𝒜 corbeled brick base raises this fireplace above floor level. The pre-built heat-circu-
lating unit is contained in a simple mass of brickwork, accented by the
addition of a horizontal row of low-wattage accent lights. Brick drops
back from the main face to wrap the pre-built metal flue system.

Figure 86. Contemporary fireplace design.

This design combines rough stone, copper, and wood paneled walls. The thin, project-ing hearth and mantel are covered with sheet copper. The recessed area above the mantel has copper ribs applied to the face of sheet copper.

Figure 87. Contemporary fireplace design.

A simple brick mass defines this fireplace with the brick laid in "stacked" bond pattern. Thick wood creates the mantel and log storage areas, while thinner woodwork forms the upper mantel shelf and bookcases. A horizontal chair rail on the wall helps balance the effect of the vertical brickwork.

Figure 88. Contemporary fireplace design.

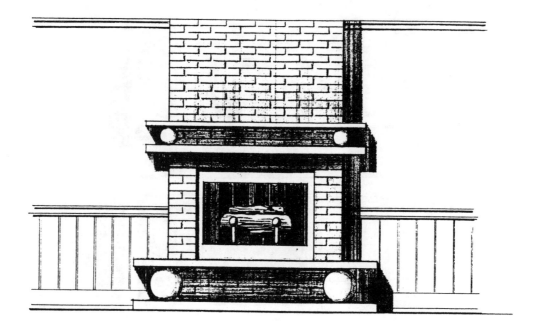

$\mathcal{A}$ *simple brick fireplace takes on a different look with the hearth and mantel treatment in this design. Spheres of metal, stone, or wood separate and help support the two slabs of the hearth. The slabs can again be of metal or stone. The theme is echoed in the mantel at a smaller and lighter scale.*

Figure 89. Contemporary fireplace design.

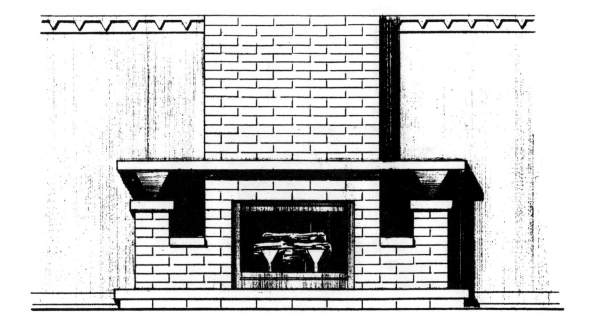

Stone slabs and inverted pyramids combine with simple brickwork for a unique effect. The same components could be of built-up construction and covered with copper or steel. The low, raised hearth gives a strong horizontal line, as does the mantel. The shape of the inverted pyramids supporting the ends of the mantel is repeated in the layered wood ceiling trim.

Figure 90. Contemporary fireplace design.

Segmented wood columns support the raised hearth and mantel and extend to the ceiling. Brick houses the pre-built unit. The pre-built flue is wrapped by a larger diameter metal tube, which is painted to match the decor. The actual hearth and mantel can be of cast white concrete, or they can be built up and covered with metal. The mantel could be created with wood. The inset panels of the wainscot echo the curves of mantel and hearth.

Figure 91. Contemporary fireplace design.

The pre-built heat-circulating unit is contained in brickwork, which features an arch form. The brick stops below ceiling level, and the pre-built flue is contained within a larger diameter metal tube of painted metal or sheet copper. The center inset displays a carved wood fan design. Post lights complete the design.

Figure 92. Contemporary fireplace design.

Simple dark brickwork provides the face of this conventional fireplace. The mantel is of smooth, cast white concrete, as is the inset panel above the mantel. These elements could also be built up from other materials and surfaced with finish materials or created with wood.

Figure 93. Contemporary fireplace design.

The mantel with its curves can be fabricated by bending or building up wood. The basic conventional fireplace is of brick. The center panel can be surface-carved or feature painted design.

Figure 94. Contemporary fireplace design.

Tapered wood columns and a thick wood mantel balance the vertical fireplace element of stack-bond brick. The raised brick hearth provides a strong horizontal base for the whole assembly. Metal molding surrounds the actual firebox.

Figure 95. Contemporary fireplace design.

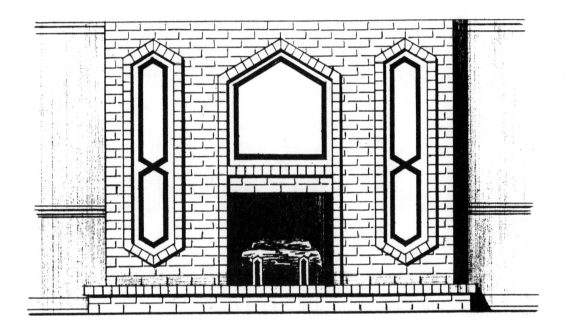

This conventional fireplace has its brick surface punctuated with inset panels. The panels can be of wood, drywall, or plaster. The linear designs on the panels can be painted or formed with moldings for a three-dimensional effect.

Figure 96. Island-type see-through fireplace design.

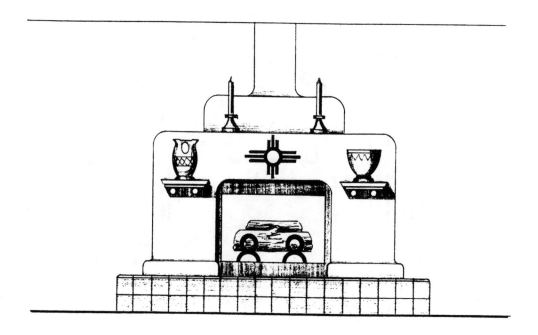

Intended to stand alone, this see-through fireplace uses a pre-built unit. The stepped stucco fireplace stands on a raised hearth with quarry tile surface and faces. The pre-built flue is contained in a larger square-shaped stuccoed enclosure. Small wood shelves rest on projecting wood dowels.

Figure 97. Island-type see-through fireplace design.

$\mathcal{S}$tone creates this see-through fireplace with its raised hearth. It houses a pre-built unit. The wood mantel is balanced by the two smaller wood elements, which separate the tall opening at the right side into three segments. The bottom opening serves as storage for firewood. The single pendant light and hanging fire tools add interest.

Figure 98. Island-type see-through (all four sides) fireplace design.

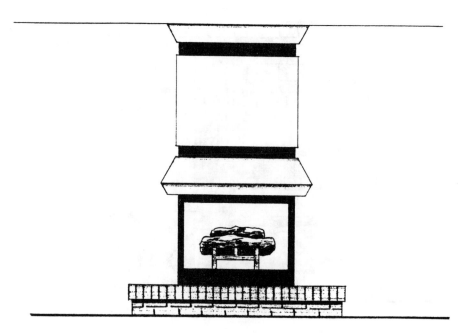

In this design, the fire is visible from front, back, and both sides since it uses a pre-built unit designed for that purpose. It rests on a raised brick hearth. The upper portion has faceted faces and can be created with metal or a combination of metal and stucco.

Figure 99. Island-type see-through (all four sides) fireplace design.

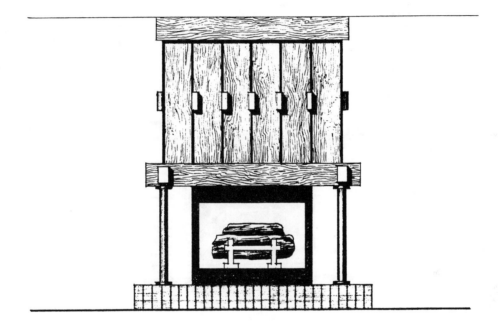

*R*ustic wood, a raised hearth of brick, and steel columns at its four corners combine for this see-through fireplace. A pre-built unit permits viewing the fire from all four sides as it stands between rooms or in the center of a room.

Figure 100. Corner-type fireplace design.

Uncut stone provides the face for this corner fireplace with its pre-built unit. The mantel and its side supports are heavy milled planks. The raised hearth has a cut stone slab as its surface. The slab could be of pre-cast concrete or built up with wood components and surfaced with tile.

Figure 101. Corner-type fireplace design.

The flowing lines of this stucco corner fireplace are contrasted with the quarry tile floor surface adjacent to the raised hearth. The basic construction relies on concrete or lightweight concrete block, which provides the base surface for the stucco.

Figure 102. Corner-type fireplace design.

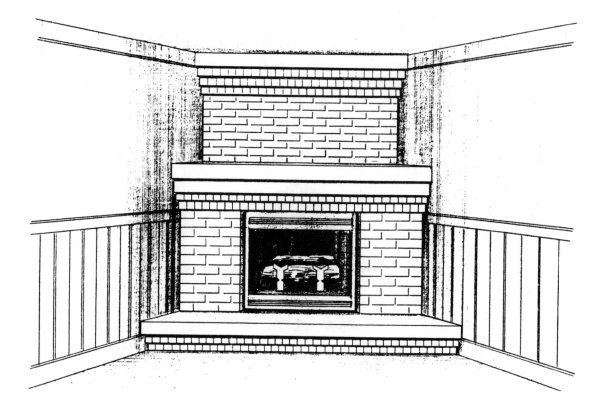

A corner fireplace, this design combines brick with slabs of cut stone for hearth, mantel, and top trim. The mantel, hearth, and top trim could be built up from other materials and simply surfaced with wood as long as the hearth surface was covered with a non-combustible material such as tile.

Figure 103. Corner-type fireplace design.

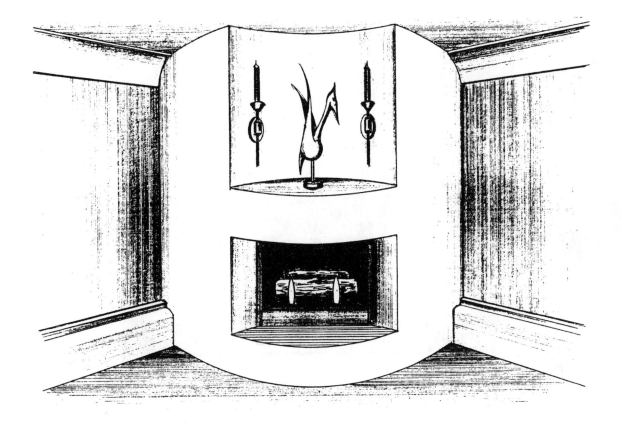

*S*haped plaster ceiling coves and wall bases complement the cylindrical shape of this corner fireplace. The pre-built unit is enclosed in a structure faced with stucco. The hearth is shown with a ribbed metal surface. The projecting area above the firebox should have its bottom surface covered with that same material. The curved recessed area above the mantel ledge provides opportunities for display of sculpture.

Figure 104. Corner-type fireplace design.

A metal, or stuccoed, hood tops the brick of this corner fireplace. The pre-built unit rests on a full-width raised hearth with its two recesses for log storage. The hearth could be topped with a slab of cut stone or cast concrete, or built up with wood and covered with tile.

Figure 105. Corner-type fireplace design.

Simple brick encloses the pre-built unit of this corner fireplace. The low raised hearth can be stone, cast concrete, or wood covered with tile or decorative sheet metal. The cylindrical hood is fabricated from metal. The main surface is sheet copper, and the trim is copper or painted steel.

Conclusion

*T*his book is intended to develop a basic understanding of the evolution of fireplaces, how fireplaces work, methods by which they can be constructed, components available, types of pre-built units currently on the market, how codes affect fireplace construction, and factors to consider when obtaining or purchasing firewood. Certainly, one of the book's most important purposes is to provide a reasonably broad range of ideas for the finished appearance of fireplaces.

Many sources have more detailed information available regarding the mechanical aspects of installing specific components and manufactured units. Much of this material is furnished at no charge to potential purchasers. Such sources include general contractors, lumber yards, building materials centers, home improvement centers, and fireplace and fireplace equipment dealers.

It is to be hoped that no one considers a fireplace to require no care or maintenance. Also on a hopeful note, no one holds the thought that a cheerful crackling wood fire appears magically, with no effort on the part of the fireplace owners. Admittedly, fireplaces are not appropriate for everyone, nor are they appropriate for all dwellings. For those who can utilize a fireplace, the author truly believes that its benefits far outweigh the efforts required in its care and feeding. If this book has helped others in reaching the same conclusion, it has been a successful project, worthy of the time and effort expended in its creation.

Glossary

ANDIRONS—Originally two vertical bars on flat or arched leg bases, with an elevated cross-brace to space them and keep them upright. Firewood is placed on or leaned against the cross-brace. Now mainly used as a decorative item.

ASH DUMP—A metal opening with a sliding top. Ashes fall through the ash dump into the ash pit.

ASH LIP—A raised section at the front of the firebox hearth.

ASH PIT—A hollow, masonry-enclosed space below the firebox. Ashes can be dumped into the space for disposal later. Also called ASH DUMP.

BACK HEARTH—The portion of the hearth inside the firebox. Often the term HEARTH is used alone.

CHIMNEY—The structure, often masonry, enclosing the flue, which drafts smoke up and away from the firebox.

CONVECTION—Heat transfer by air circulation.

CORD—The standard measure for firewood: 128 cubic feet, or 8 feet long, 4 feet wide, and 4 feet high. See also SHORT CORD, FACE CORD.

COUNT RUMFORD FIREPLACE—The type of fireplace designed by Benjamin Thompson, Count Rumford.

CRANE—An arm of metal designed to pivot over the fire to support the handle of a kettle or cooking pot.

DAMPER—A metal plate used to control the draft in a fireplace.

EXTENDED HEARTH—The portion of the hearth that extends into the room. Also called FRONT HEARTH.

FACE CORD—A smaller quantity of firewood than a cord, the face cord is 8 feet long and 4 feet high, but the length of the logs can vary. Log length is usually 16, 20, or 24 inches. Also called SHORT CORD.

FIREBOX—The space in the fireplace that contains the fire.

FIREBRICK—A durable brick used in firebox construction. It has less tendency to crack and deteriorate from intense heat than does regular brick.

FIRESTOP—Non-combustible material, usually sheet metal, placed between the chimney or flue and any surrounding combustible material.

FLUE—The passage for smoke through a chimney.

FLUE LINER—The material, fired-clay or metal pipe, used to line a flue.

FRANKLIN STOVE — A cast iron stove designed by Benjamin Franklin.

FRONT HEARTH—The portion of the hearth extending into the room. Also called EXTENDED HEARTH.

GRATE—A frame of metal bars used to hold fuel in a fireplace.

HEARTH—The bottom of the firebox.

HEARTH EXTENSION—The portion of the hearth that extends into the room. Also called EXTENDED HEARTH.

HEAT-CIRCULATING FIREPLACE—A double-walled fireplace unit installed on a non-combustible firebrick hearth and surrounded with two layers of common brick (or one layer of common brick and one layer of face brick). It has a clay-tile flue liner surrounded by brick, and incorporates firebox, throat, damper, smoke shelf, and smoke dome in a single pre-built unit.

HIGH-FORMED DAMPER—A damper that also provides the throat and permits a deeper smoke shelf.

ISLAND FIREPLACE—A rectangular fireplace unit with the fire visible from all four sides.

KITCHEN RANGE—A cast iron, wood-fired stove.

LINTEL — A horizontal architectural member supporting the brick, stone, or other material over the fireplace.

MANTEL — The component framing the fireplace opening. Usually only serving a decorative purpose.

POTBELLY STOVE—A cast iron wood-burning stove.

RADIATION—Heat reflected from glowing embers and flames bouncing off the sides and back of the fireplace.

RAISED HEARTH—A hearth above floor level.

REFRACTORY—Able to withstand high temperatures.

RUMFORD FIREPLACE — The type of fireplace designed by Benjamin Thompson, Count Rumford.

SHORT CORD — A smaller quantity of firewood than a cord, the short cord is 8 feet long and 4 feet high, but the length of the logs can vary. Log length is usually 16, 20, or 24 inches. Also called FACE CORD.

SMOKE CHAMBER — The space from the top of the throat to the bottom of the flue.

SMOKE DOME—The smoke chamber of a prefabricated fireplace unit.

SMOKE LOUVERS—Hollow ventilated devices used to control the effects of wind on the fireplace and to protect from rain.

SMOKE SHELF—A horizontal shelf the same width as the throat and extending from the back of the throat to the back of the flue.

SPARK CAP—A unit above the top of the flue designed to prevent downdrafts and to shed rainwater. Some spark caps incorporate a metal mesh screen to prevent sparks from leaving the flue.

SPIT—A horizontal rod used for cooking meat and hanging pots over a fire.

SURROUND—The area on the front surface of the fireplace, adjacent to the sides and top of the firebox.

THROAT—The opening, or passage, from the firebox to the smoke chamber.

WALL FIREPLACE—A fireplace built or placed against a wall.

ZERO CLEARANCE FIREPLACE—A factory-built metal fireplace unit.

Index